W9-ABP-513

CONFLICT IN COMMUNITY

CONFLICT IN COMMUNITY

by

Robert J. McAllister, Ph.D., M.D.

IMH

INSTITUTE FOR MENTAL HEALTH
St. John's University Press
Collegeville, Minnesota

Library of Congress Catalog Card Number: 77-83089

PRINTED IN THE UNITED STATES OF AMERICA

To all religious women —

by vow and by disposition —

but especially to Jane

Preface

As a behavioral scientist, a psychiatrist and psychologist, Robert McAllister brings a deep knowledge of human behavior and development to his studies of the problems encountered by women who live religious life. His knowledge, combined with broad experience in working with, talking to, and treating religious men and women has enabled him to evaluate objectively and sensitively the psychological strengths and weaknesses of the life itself and of the individuals who choose to live it. Throughout this book, one is struck by the understanding which he has of human nature in general and of the stresses which that human nature must meet in a religious congregation. One also recognizes in Dr. McAllister a sensitivity to persons, a concern for persons and respect of the individual, along with an awareness of the weaknesses and fallibilities inherent in any man.

With the great changes in religious life today, the need for an open discussion of the demands such a life places on an individual is greater than ever before. Structures, rules, regulations, and even the so-called practices of the life are being questioned, modified, and in some cases, completely eliminated. This has led to an uncovering, as it were, of serious flaws within the life and of serious weaknesses in some individuals who live it. While causing deep concern to those who have a high regard for the true nature of this life, this uncovering has also given them hope that the future will be brighter. For those who are discovering their own weaknesses, it enables them to work out, for themselves, a healthy and realistic way of coping with the pressures of religious life. This, in turn, will make this kind of life a source of spiritual joy and meaning to them, as well as a benefit to the Church and the people of God whom they serve. This greater awareness of themselves and deeper appreciation for the real nature of religious life will lead to a greater regard for the worth and beauty of every individual, religious and lay.

In his chapter on the assessment of candidates for religious life, Dr. McAllister emphasizes this need for respect for the person, and suggests that psychological tests and evaluations be used more for the benefit of the candidate than for that of the congregation. Major superiors should read and reread this particular chapter, since it is an excellent summary of the true value of psychological testing and purpose.

Those chapters discussing the effect of family life on the individual, self-image and acceptance, and the stresses found in religious life offer valuable helps to those who counsel and direct others toward religious life as well as to those who are entrusted with the development of the young women who choose it. In these chapters there is a wealth of information presented in a clear and lucid way. Even for those who have a good background in psychology, the material, as presented, offers new insights into the human personality. Dr. McAllister has had a thorough academic training in both psychology and psychiatry, which he has used to good purpose in his actual dealings with people.

While one might disagree with some of the ideas expressed by Dr. McAllister in his chapter on feminine fulfillment (seeing in it the traditional viewpoint of a man), one must agree with him as he discusses love in religious life and the psychology of community. These chapters will help all religious to develop a greater understanding of their own needs and expectations and should do much to help them live more peacefully with themselves and others.

This book, which discusses so clearly and unambiguously the psychological problems encountered in religious life, comes at a time when it is needed by many religious. It is written in language which is both scholarly and poetic and so is appealing to the intelligent and idealistic women who will benefit from it. It has been a pleasure and honor for me to read it and to recommend it to other religious, as well as to anyone concerned with religious life.

Sister Sarah Louise O'Brien, M.D.

Contents

CHAPTER

I Screening Candidates for the Religious Life . . . 3

II Family Life and Its Effect on Personality . . . 13

III Self Image and Self Acceptance 24

IV The Psychology of Community 35

V Stress in the Religious Life 46

VI Anxiety in the Religious Life 54

VII Psychosomatic Illness in the Religious Life . . . 66

VIII Anger in the Religious Life 77

IX Love in the Religious Life 89

X Fulfillment of the Feminine Personality in the Religious Life 101

Introduction

"Community" has become one of those magic words with definitions, meanings and nuances not covered in standard dictionaries. Webster's definitions of "community" do not include the meaning of the term as used by many religious.

It is not uncommon today for a religious woman to return to her motherhouse or local convent after spending several months at school or at a workshop and announce, "We really had community this summer." Likewise, it is not uncommon to hear the comment from a group of Sisters who are revising their constitutions or involved in a self-evaluation, "We have no community in our convent."

In the above uses, "to have community" is considered the highest compliment, and "to lack community" is a severe criticism. This use of the word "community" by persons who are living in the same place, under the same laws, belonging to the same organization, and having common interests refers to a dimension beyond the ordinary definition. What it implies is a reverence for, or search for, or appreciation of, a psychological dimension to common living.

Dr. Robert McAllister proposed some of the ideas in this book at a conference for religious women at St. Benedict's Convent in St. Joseph, Minnesota. His thoughts are on some essential elements of a stable, effective group of women living together in the religious life. He deals with some of the important psychological dimensions of community living.

To "have community" in its current sense, there must be opportunities with the group for the fulfillment of normal dependency needs. The group must provide the security in which the members can relax and feel capable of honestly expressing themselves and their needs.

Members of the group should know each other well enough to react spontaneously to each other if group members are to have the opportunity for the fulfillment of normal needs. This kind of spontaneous awareness of other members of the group involves a realistic mutual acceptance.

Feelings of hostility will inevitably arise in any group of people living together because of differences in background, values and perspectives. To establish group living, there must be opportunities for the acceptance of the hostilities which arise. There are many religious who resist the idea that hostilities are inevitable in group living. But is it possible to have a group of people needing and sustaining one another without also resenting one another at times?

If there is no room for hostility, there will be no room for reparation. This is one reason why there must be opportunities for the acceptance of hostility within a community. The attempt to avoid all expressions of hostility only compounds misunderstanding. The acknowledgment of hostilities, on the other hand, can lead to clarification and deeper understanding.

Community ought to foster each Sister's sense of self-sufficiency. Each member ought to have her "place" and her area of responsibility. No member of a group possesses all the strength or all the weakness. A group that "has community" will accept the Sister as she is and allow her to grow.

No significant or lasting relationship can exist without the acceptance of responsibility. In fulfilling one's responsibilities to the group, one defines his ideals and goals, and finds freedom within real limits. The security and stability of the community are founded on each member's sense of responsible commitment to the group as a whole.

One of the dangers in community life is to "missanctify" either objects or persons. Missanctification confuses accidentals with essentials. If no better reason can be found for a rule or custom than "It's the way we have always done it," that rule or custom should possibly be abandoned. The religious woman attempts to achieve a feeling of self-worth by surrounding herself, as it were, with holy things. This thinking, although common, is not far removed from the child's belief that in holding or possessing an object of special merit he will receive some magic power.

A kind of magic can be invested in a person also – often the novice mistress or superior. A community member can idealize one of the members of the group. This is an attempt to derive strength by association. Of course the pitfalls are obvious.

Viewed dynamically, the family is a structure in which the parents foster growth in order that their children may achieve full maturity and independence. Religious communities often view themselves statically and establish structures that will perpetuate the relationship of parents and dependent children. In such a community a Sister feels that she would be helpless without the community. She also feels a loss if the strong members, whom she tends to view as parental figures, disapprove of her.

This kind of community-family encourages competitive struggles with all their attendant pains and pleasures. Love and support are meted out "to keep the children happy." Control within such a community is established, not by love nor by dedication nor by a reasoned response to human needs, but by guilt. Jealousy and pettiness are unconsciously fostered within the community. The psychological and spiritual hangovers from Manicheanism, Puritanism, pietism – call them what you will – remain active in these communities that foster immature dependency, unhealthy competition, and related feelings of guilt.

Conflicts in community are inevitable. Hopefully most conflicts will arise out of, and contribute to, the process of growth and maturation. Dr. McAllister's book is presented to make that goal possible – that "community" may exist in our religious communities.

A. W. R. Sipe

CONFLICT IN COMMUNITY

CHAPTER I

SCREENING CANDIDATES FOR THE RELIGIOUS LIFE

Before considering the problems of screening candidates for the religious life, there is a question which should properly be raised: why screen candidates for the religious life? Screening has become a password in our modern society – and it is literally a password – for screening opens up doors to the "good guys," the ones who are on the side of right and goodness and all that America stands for. It also closes the doors on the "bad guys," those who see things a bit differently, those who sometimes cannot be identified other than by the fact that they did not pass the test.

There is, indeed, a new breed in religion. There is, in a sense, a new brand of religion that hastens to make use of all the modern implements that science offers, from high speed electronic computers to high pressure business consultants to sometimes high-handed screening techniques. Before evaluating the techniques of screening, it is appropriate to look at the philosophy of screening candidates for the religious life.

Why screen candidates? There are three possible answers: screen for the sake of the common good, i.e. society; screen for the sake of the community; or screen for the sake of the applicant. Which of these is the proper philosophy of screening?

If the philosophy of screening involves the common good – for example, the possibility of scandal due to delinquent behavior – this seems to be a reasonable basis for employing the techniques. If communities are concerned that a Sister who becomes schizophrenic may provide an unhealthy climate for children in her classroom, if superiors are apprehensive that a Sister who uses alcohol or who acts out sexually may become a stumbling block for others on the path to heaven, then they may justifiably desire techniques to prevent such people from entering the religious life.

If screening is done for the good of the community, one is on quite different ground. Superiors may say that the emotionally disturbed will cause unhappiness to others in the community. In truth, they cause unhappiness to others wherever they are and in many different ways, but they cannot be eliminated from the face of the earth. Superiors may say that the community cannot afford to provide the psychiatric care the emotionally disturbed may need. What does a wife with five small children do when her husband needs to go to a psychiatrist? This philosophy of selection seems to be a tenuous one. Isn't it possible that God might give a vocation to someone who is not very stable emotionally? After all, it is assumed that he gives the vocation of marriage to some who have all kinds of physical and emotional disabilities. Look through the pages of Church history; read Scripture itself. Is there any evidence that God picked only the best, only the most stable individuals to do his work? Why must religious communities be so careful in selecting only the best? Or is that not the purpose of some selection programs?

The final philosophy of screening is undoubtedly the most sound because it has as its focus the good of the individual who is being tested. It has as its purpose the future happiness and possibly the ultimate salvation of that individual. If a selection program is based on the premise of trying to help a person find out whether or not she will be suited to and content in the religious life, then testing and evaluation serve their highest functions. The integrity of the individual is preserved, and the community serves the providential and inscrutable will of God. This is a solid basis for using selection methods.

Based on the latter philosophy there are practical purposes which screening may serve. One might properly think of it as a kind of abbreviated novitiate, for the answers which are being sought in such a program are really answers to the same questions that are being asked in novitiate. How will this individual adapt to community living? What emotional conflicts will this way of life create? What problems may occur for this individual in terms of the religious life? These are the types of questions which are appropriately involved in any screening program for religious. These are also questions which can be presumed to be an important aspect of the period of novitiate. The questions may be worded differently. The community asks the psychological or psychiatric evaluator how emotionally stable is this candidate and, an even more important question, how emotionally stable is this individual likely to remain if she enters religion. In the novitiate the community asks how worthy a candidate is this religious and how good a religious will she become. In the latter question the spiritual development is emphasized, in the former question the emotional maturity is emphasized. There are those who maintain that spiritual development depends on emotional maturity. Although there is reason to doubt the universal validity of this relationship, there certainly is, in the practical forum, a close association between the two facets of an individual's development.

There follows, from these statements, an obvious question: is the screening procedure or is the novitiate more likely to answer the questions more accurately? There are two major limitations in any screening program. First, there is no test or group of tests, no evaluative techniques, which can accurately predict future behavior. One is, at best, dealing in statistical verities which fall short in accurately describing the specific individual. Secondly, psychological testing and interviewing techniques cannot predict or even begin to fathom the influence which a life in religion may have on the individual.

There are many intangibles associated with a religious commitment and many imponderables associated with the dedication of a religious. There are also many unknown graces associated with the religious life. All of these remain unknown in the dynamic equation which reads: this individual plus the religious life equals benefit or detriment. Screening can only concern itself directly with the individual; it can do little to understand how religious life will affect him.

Will the novitiate better answer these questions? Yes, it would seem so. The burden of decision which should rest in the novitiate may be gradually shifting to psychological testing and psychiatric evaluation. There is no better assurance of admitting suitable persons to the religious life than to have well-trained, carefully chosen, novice mistresses, women who have enough broad experience to appreciate the beauty of rough stones. They should have enough humility and humor to recognize their own delusions and distortions, enough courage to encourage others to seek their happiness outside the religious life when it seems so indicated. It is only in the novitiate that the complete formula is present: the individual plus the life of community and of dedication.

This is the real crucible for testing vocations. Only a sensitive, patient, prudent individual can look into another's heart with understanding and appreciation. This cannot occur during psychological testing or some brief psychiatric interviewing.

There is no intention of completely dissuading superiors from the notion of testing candidates. It is important to emphasize these few points, because it would appear at times that the worldliness of testing may displace the wisdom of the novice mistresses and superiors. There is considerable misgiving creeping into our society regarding the use of psychological tests, psychiatric interviews and lie detector tests to assess applicants for positions in government and private industry. There is a clamor arising against the encroachment on personal privacy which these methods imply. Prying into minds may produce results which were not anticipated. It would be ironical if all the research necessary to validate the various tests for each religious community were completed, and soon afterward a law were passed forbidding the use of such measures to discriminate with regard to job placement.

There is a place for screening, even though it has been pushed further and further from the scene. Some basic principles should be kept in mind. What does the community expect to get from these screening techniques? What are those who do the screening promising? The expectations of the community are one thing; those who provide the screening may have different expectations. It is important that the community and the professionals who screen do not speak different languages. Otherwise, confusion is certain to result. Even worse, some worthy candidate may get lost in the gap between communication levels.

What can be reasonably expected of a screening program? One can expect some fairly accurate estimate of the emotional health of the individual in question. (This is the same as one can expect from a medical doctor with regard to the question of the physical health of an individual.) One can expect to get an accurate appraisal of the intelligence level of a candidate. These two items are really the substance of what can be expected. There may be refinements describing the personality or the psychological attributes of the individual or the relative strength or weakness of her various intellectual traits.

There is a crucial point. Neither the psychologist nor the psychiatrist, any more than the general practitioner of medicine, should be asked or expected to decide whether this woman should be a sister. This is a decision any one of these professionals is unqualified to make. On the other hand, any one of these professionals might properly discuss with a religious candidate the pros and cons of religious life for her, considering the facts of her intellectual level, her personality characteristics, and her state of physical health. Following the screening, there are only two sources of a "yes" or "no" answer with regard to the question of a vocation. One source is the prospective candidate, who can say she does or does not want to be a sister. The other source is the representative of that particular religious community who also must say "yes" or "no" to the possibility of this person becoming a member.

By the same token, becoming a religious involves positive response by both of these parties, not just one. When a community places its decision in the hands of a consultant psychologist or psychiatrist it is shirking its responsibility, just as the candidate who puts her decision in the hands of the mistress of novices is shirking her basic responsibility.

What can those who are involved in the screening program expect to give to the community? They can give an honest evaluation of the individual candidate with due recognition of the limits of their own techniques and the fallibility of their own judgments. Superiors being conscious of their own fallibility have perhaps turned to scientific assessment in the hope of ridding themselves of the risk of error. Those who do this type of personality assessment, or any kind of personality assessment, should be ever aware of their own limitations. This dependency on scientific techniques is used in various government agencies. One of the most difficult tasks which the evaluators have to do is to convince the authorities that they, as evaluators, have definite limitations. In their desire to feel secure in their security measures, the authorities constantly look for infallibility. The mystery which seems to surround psychiatry provides them with the opportunity to deceive themselves into thinking that here may be the answer. Sometimes psychologists and psychiatrists become a bit enamored of their own profession and lose perspective on themselves, giving rise to a feeling of omnipotence. In their desire to serve (which is a charitable interpretation) or in their desire to be omnipotent (which is a less charitable interpretation), they cannot resist the temptation to give answers to questions which others so confidently and so properly ask of them. And the question becomes: should this young woman be a nun?

It is truely awesome to contemplate the profundity of the choices that will alter the entire course of one's future life and most certainly effect the settlement of one's eternity. It seems so rash, so ill-advised, so utterly presumptuous to attempt to make such a decision for another human being, even if one makes it only in a negative manner by denying that person the opportunity to make the positive choice. When the community makes a choice not to accept a person, it is making somewhat the same choice as a young man or woman does who chooses not to marry a certain person. In such a case the young man is not denying the girl's right to marry, he is simply stating his unwillingness to accept her as *his* bride. But the psychologist, the psychiatrist, and even the religious authority is playing the role of God when he says this person should or should not be a religious. Who has the right to deny the individual the right to marry or the right to become a religious? This is not as simple a question as it may seem. Its answer must be seriously considered before screening programs can be justified in their use as absolute criteria for acceptance or rejection.

There are various devices and methods that are used in screening programs. The simplest method is the questionnaire. This has been used for decades by many religious communities. Perhaps they were not aware that they were assessing personality. They asked such questions as: "Are your parents separated, is either parent an alcoholic, were you ever expelled from school?" The only practical reason for asking such questions was to gather some information about this candidate. The underlying assumption was that such items of past experience would have an effect on the personality of the individual.

Questionnaires have become more elaborate. A well-devised questionnaire can provide a great deal of knowledge about the prospective candidate. This is perhaps the most crude of the screening devices but it should not be discounted. A questionnaire is inexpensive to produce and can be informative in a very direct way. In other words, it gives valuable information which need not be interpreted by the professional psychologist, who adds only one more fallible link in the chain. The questionnaire is especially useful if the community authorities are going to keep their decision-making role and not pass it on to the professionals.

A second measure of emotional stability is the battery of psychological tests. There are many tests which can be used and many which are used by various psychologists in various ways. One warning must be given. These tests — no matter how good they are, no matter how many there are — are also not infallible. Their validity is based generally on their applicability to large populations. They are as reliable as statistics, no more so. (Should a community refuse admission to a particular candidate because she is 45 years old and has blue eyes and blond hair, if it had been proved statistically that only 1% of such candidates remain in the religious life?) Some tests are certainly more valid than others and therefore more useful. Most professionals would probably agree that the MMPI or Minnesota Multiphasic Personality Inventory would be the most useful single test as a routine screening device for candidates.

In addition a general test of intelligence would seem to be appropriate. A battery of tests to be given to every candidate could be devised by a consulting psychologist. Such tests could be useful in picking out candidates who might need further intensive investigation. In other words, the tests should not be used to refuse admission to candidates but only to suggest more careful consideration of them before admission. The next logical step might be individual psychological testing of the doubtfuls. This should involve testing with projective tests such as the Rorschach and Thematic Apperception Test. However, a community should be cautious about refusing a candidate on the basis of these tests alone. Superiors must not be led to believe that these psychological tests probe into the hidden recesses of the mind and accurately reveal information which would be unavailable otherwise. These tests only give information which could be obtained by observation and interview, but the tests may arrive at the information more quickly. They do not give a new kind of information.

Test results also suggest to the psychologist hypotheses regarding this person's adaptive mechanisms. These hypotheses are often corroborated in a later interview. The best psychologists use testing to suggest such hypotheses or to corroborate hypotheses which have already been formulated regarding the person's personality. An important point becomes evident. The psychologist relies heavily on the clinical interview for his final evaluation. This means, of course, that the tests are no better than the psychologist administering them. They are only adjunctive to the clinical interview conducted by the testing psychologist.

If individual psychological testing suggests some candidate is not well suited to the religious life, the decision to admit or not to admit her should not rest on this evidence alone. In the hierarchy of screening techniques the psychiatric interview would then be in order. It is the psychiatrist and not the psychologist who is best equipped to conduct a personality evaluation by means of clinical interview. His particular training and his professional experience make him the one best qualified to do this job.

It is in this interview evaluation that family background and early childhood experiences can be examined for their proper significance. Only through such interviewing can one come to any appreciation of the relationship which this candidate had with her father and mother and siblings, relationships which will indubitably affect her relationships with the authority of superiors in the convent and with the sibling situations reduplicated in her contacts with peer religious. During the interview these family influences can be traced through her years of development as a child into the tumultuous years of teen-age trials. The balance of security and struggle, of guidance and spontaneity, of discipline and independence can be studied in a quick analysis of home and school adjustment. Incidents of childhood which may have had a lasting traumatic effect may be discovered in the course of such an evaluation. Relationships outside the family circle become important as the child gradually develops beyond the confines of that first protective community. Her acceptance of responsibility in terms of school life, neighborhood activities, and social activities suitable for her age all indicate various aspects of the maturity of her personality.

In this assessment the psychiatrist is interested in how the individual manages her emotional life. The degree of anxiety is considered, as is the manner in which anxiety is expressed and controlled. An important aspect of such an evaluation is to discover how the candidate gets angry, indeed whether or not the candidate is even aware of becoming angry, how she deals with her anger, and what guilt she may feel in relation to it. The psychiatrist would also wish to know how the candidate regards her own sexuality, both as a quality of her womanhood and also as a quantity of force to be reckoned with.

General questions of health and sickness should be raised. What illnesses has the candidate had, what operations, what injuries? Even more important, how has she reacted to sickness? Has she capitalized on every illness to gain sympathy, to get out of work around the home, to miss school? Has she had frequent illnesses suggesting psychosomatic etiology? What is her philosophy of pain? These questions are part of a psychiatric evaluation.

This type of evaluation by the psychiatrist may take several interviews. The number should be left to his discretion. He should be expected to send a report on the results to the community authorities. The report should give some indication of the personality strengths and weaknesses of the individual and should also attempt some kind of prediction as to her chances of maintaining her emotional stability in the religious life.

However, this report is only a consultative one. The decision to reject a candidate must rest with the community authorities. In this regard they should not feel bound by the reports of their consultants but remember the fallibility of all.

There is one best criterion of personality strengths and weaknesses which is used extensively by the various military and civilian agencies of the government which must select their cadre of personnel as carefully as possible. This best single criterion is the past performance of the individual. Human behavior will always be difficult to predict. But even though they will continue to do the unpredictable, it is precisely because humans do the predictable the majority of the time that we take notice when they vary from the predictable pattern. It is because the child is father of the man that we become so interested in his early adjustment in the home and in school. This does have a predictive value. The use of this criterion in selecting candidates for the religious life is limited because those entering the convent usually do so at a fairly early age. This limits the period of past performance which can be considered in making an evaluation. Frequently candidates have hardly settled down following the turmoil of teen years before they are placed in the crucible of the convent. Some communities insist that candidates wait a few years after completion of high school before entering the novitiate. The younger the candidate the less certitude there will be in screening programs. The limitation of age also means that some considerable maturation must still take place in the young candidate in question. Can this maturation process occur during novitiate? If so, then novitiate must be such an experience that maturation will be fostered and not further retarded.

The question of screening candidates for the religious life has become extremely popular. It is something of a fad which has not yet reached its apogee. If one considers it a method of assisting a candidate to know whether or not she can be content in the religious life and save her soul there, if one considers it a device to help superiors discover whether or not this candidate may get to heaven through the narrow doors of this community, if one bears in mind that science can assist the work of the Holy Spirit but never contain it, if one is mindful of the individual's own obligation in regard to decisions, then psychological and psychiatric evaluation can prove a boon to the future success of a community. One side effect of such evaluation that should not be discounted is that some candidates will be found who need psychiatric help at the time, and who, following such psychiatric help or concomitant with it, can become happy and useful religious, profitable to themselves, to the community, and to the Lord.

As a final note, it is profitable to remember that some saints, some founders of communities, some of today's religious would not have been and would not be in the religious life had these screening techniques been applied rigidly. One can imagine how a psychological report might have disagreed with some of our Lord's choices. The psychological summation on St. Peter might have read:

"Has good intelligence but is a low achiever – spends his time fishing. Shows evidence of capacity for violence. This, coupled with poor impulse control, makes him a bad risk. He might impulsively use a dangerous weapon, such as a sword, against another."

The psychologist might have quoted his report on Judas and said, "See, I told you so." His report might have read, "Is basically an anal character with characteristic patterns of avarice and obsessional behavior. When his defenses break down, he becomes depressed. Tendencies toward suicide."

The report on St. John might have been most discouraging: "Possesses a good intellect and has good ability in interpersonal relationships. There are, however, indications of homosexual tendencies."

If candidates for marriage were screened in such manner, undoubtedly many of them would not be allowed to marry. If this were true, surely some of us would not be here, for our own good parents may have had their deficiencies of intellect, their instabilities of emotion; but God chose them to bring into the world creatures such as us, whom he can somehow have the patience to love.

CHAPTER II

FAMILY LIFE AND ITS EFFECT ON PERSONALITY

The softness of a mother's hand caresses the head of her crying infant and peace comes to both of them. The strength of a father's arm embraces the shoulder of his restless child and they are content. The tear that tells of a bruised knee or a broken toy floods the heart of a parent with concern and care. The smile that dances in the eyes of a delighted infant illumines the dusk of a parent's duties and touches his soul with gladness.

The warmth of a caress, the understanding of an embrace, the press of concern, the response of joy – all of these become part of that almost mystical phenomenon which has been called personality. So many of life's great mysteries, of life's complex moments, are known through the simplicity of a single word. That single word may be used so frequently that it becomes common.

Modern civilization has become engrossed in the study of space. Through the popularization of scientific data, people who gazed at God's heavens of sky and stars with their natural eyes now visualize with the eyes of science man's heavens of radio waves and radiation belts. They are duly impressed by the beauty of the great galaxies and the complexities of the solar system.

Yet, within each human being there is such a complicated system, an intricate combination of forces with such a reservoir of power, that it defies complete analysis or adequate description. A human personality has not existed for eons of time, as have the heavenly systems. It is not shrouded in darkness behind the veil of time or separated from study by the enchanted abyss of space. The personality of a child develops before one's very eyes with each passing day, each moment of life. Although the child is so near one can touch him, so tiny one can pick him up with one hand, so helpless others must constantly care for him, he is not fully understood. His personality grows as his body grows. Through science we have come to understand in great detail the process of physical growth. The composition of foods is known; the nutrient needs of humans have been analyzed. The processes of assimilation that abstract from ingested foods the substances necessary for the growth and development of the human body have been charted in detail. However, one can watch the daily progress of personality formation, and still be unable to say accurately what process occurs, specifically why it occurs, or actually what ingredients go into forming this personality.

The human body has a fantastic ability to select and to assimilate what it needs for health and growth, and then to store the valuable excess as fat and discard the useless excess as waste. The process of personality growth is much more delicate, for it is much less capable of selecting what is healthy, much more vulnerable to what is harmful. It is more susceptible to undernourishment or to overloading. The warmth of maternal caresses is important to the child, but their excess can cause damage, as a tree that grows in the shadow of a great oak remains small and unhealthy. Unfortunately, the infant has no system which is psychologically selective. There is no selective screening of his experiences, as there is of food in his stomach. A baby can swallow a safety pin or a penny. If the mother is patient and the baby is lucky, she will probably get the pin or the penny back without damage or discomfort to the baby. A gentle caress, a word of encouragement, a brief unkindness, or a harsh slap cannot be recovered. They become part of the child's experience. One cannot retrieve them. One cannot even estimate their effect. If the mother does not recover the ingested pin, a doctor, with the help of x-ray, might give her some idea of how much damage it will do if it is left within the child. No one can predict the effect that an alcoholic father or a nagging mother may have on a child's personality development.

Just as the child cannot select what is best for him from his experience, so he cannot discard as waste any of the experiences which he has. There is no psychological residue. Each event in a child's life becomes part of his psychological structure. As the food he eats becomes part of the structure of his body, entering into his bones, his blood, his soft tissue, so, when he becomes an adult, the events of his childhood are still with him, affecting his personality functioning and adjustment. In fact, they form his personality.

Although it is not possible to predict accurately the effect of a single incident or even of a major psychological event on the developing personality of a child, there are some general rules to follow in building personality or, more accurately, in influencing its natural growth. Perhaps this latter distinction is the source of undue concern and unnecessary mistakes. A child's personality is not constructed by his parents or teachers. It is not built from without. It grows from within. Parents can influence that growth, they can direct it within limits, they can stimulate it, they can retard it – but grow it will! Unfortunately, parents sometimes approach the problem of rearing a child as they would approach constructing a robot.

It might be of interest to explore some of the general areas in which personality is deeply affected by parental influence and family life. To give some division to the subject, it will be of value to remember that a healthy personality must have healthy attitudes toward self, toward others, toward God, and toward the responsibilities of life. Undoubtedly, these areas overlap, so the division is somewhat artificial, but it will serve a purpose.

Of these attitudes, the most important for emotional health is that toward oneself. How does one acquire an attitude about oneself? Where does one acquire a self image, or self concept? A person is certainly not born with it. Nor is it likely that one acquires it from some intellectual self-examination and self-evaluation. Since one is not born with it, and since he does not create it within himself, he must get it from outside. He must learn it. It must come from his experience. From whom does he learn it? He learns it from his parents, from whom he learns so many things, and from whom he acquires so many attitudes about the things he learns. A child acquires an attitude about himself from the attitude his parents have about him. While this attitude toward himself may be altered by other factors later in life, its basic bent will remain that of parental persuasion.

Imagine the differences in personality in the following three examples: a wanted child born to parents anxious to have another baby, or at least accept God's providence in providing another pregnancy; a rejected child whose conception was considered a misjudgment and whose birth was considered a misfortune; an abandoned child who is raised in an orphanage or a foster home where children are numbers that can somehow be converted into dollars. Can these three children really have the same fundamental attitude about their worth as human beings? Does each one feel the same joy in the fact that he exists, the same respect for his assets as a human, the same responsibility to life, the same enthusiasm for living?

A child learns an attitude of self respect from his parents if they respect him. A family in which there is mutual respect for one another and for the individual differences and individual preferences of its members teaches a healthy self respect. Children who are allowed some specific choices from very early years learn something of their own value as individuals. If they have the freedom to get dirty, the choice of eating or not eating their spinach, the opportunity to say, "No!" and have an adult accept it, then they begin to see themselves as individuals because they see that their parents respect them as individuals. In a home where the rule of parents is strong-armed and hard-fisted, where freedom is the stepchild of rebellion, and where the only choice is to follow orders or get punished, the child learns little about his own value as an individual because he has considerable difficulty seeing himself as an individual. Isn't this the very thing which presently degrades the enslaved children of "Mother Russia?" Wasn't this the poisonous propaganda that turned Hitler's masterful horde into a dumb, obedient herd? They lost the basic respect for their own individuality, their own personal worth; and losing this, they lost respect for their fellow man, for God, for the sacredness of life.

For this reason the attitude toward self is psychologically more important than one's attitude toward one's fellow man, or toward God. Isn't this often the most difficult psychological burden of the religious life, the loss of one's individuality? There is no implication that it should be so. Sometimes in their zeal to empty themselves of self young religious forget the needs of their human nature. They forget their need to be an individual, to be different, to be oneself. Sometimes, in their desire to keep order and discipline in the house, religious superiors forget the needs of human nature. They forget the inviolability of the individual, the sacred distinctness of each of their charges. Pope John XXIII was perhaps the best modern example one could offer of the need to remain an individual; a compassionate, simple human being no matter what peaks of prestige or positions of authority one may ascend to, no matter how holy one may become.

There are two ways in which parents rob their children of individuality. The first has been mentioned, a demand for rigid adherence to ironclad rules. The second is far more subtle. In this method the child is controlled by the fear of displeasing his parents who constantly impress him with the debt of gratitude he owes them. In order not to displease them, he must try to live up to their expectations for him. As an infant, he must not disturb their sleep. As a baby, he must be toilet trained before any other child his age so his mother can boast about it. Each year, life brings new "musts". He must be first to tie his shoes, he must be the most intelligent, the most polite, the most washed, the most popular child in the neighborhood. Father comes in with his list of expectations. He must excel in sports because father did (or more likely because father did not), be popular with the girls, win a scholarship, make money.

The tragedy, of course, is that no one ever stops to ask or even to think about what this child might want. He is not an individual. He is a flag that parents wave to attract the attention of others to themselves. He is a badge they wear, and it reads, "Parents of Distinction!" He is their pawn through which they attempt to live out their frustrated dreams, or re-live their faded memories. The child grows into inert adulthood and his goal remains the same: to please his parents or some substitute parent. He never learns the task of independent decision, the value of independent thought. In a religious community, such a person functions best when mother superior reassures her continually that she is pleased with her and with her work. If mother superior forgets to do so, or does not have time, this religious is shattered and feels she is useless to the community, unworthy of her vocation, unfaithful to God.

The second set of healthy attitudes necessary for a mature personality is that which is concerned with others, others of the same sex and others of the opposite sex. Again, these attitudes are learned from the parents, who are the prototypes of male and female for their own children. Several parental attitudes are involved. First of all, the attitude of the parents toward the sex of the child is important. Maria's father, since he had no sons, strongly and obviously resented his three daughters because of their sex. Maria, in turn, grew to resent the fact that she was a girl. She found it difficult to get along with other girls, and although she tried to please the opposite sex her underlying reciprocal hostility toward her father kept her from any real rapport with them.

Secondly, the attitude of the parent toward his or her own sex also influences the child's attitudes. A father who obviously doubted his own masculinity forced his son to participate in athletics and to pick fights with other boys to prove his prowess to his father. In fact, the father was attempting to prove his own masculinity through the ability and strength of a son whom he had, after all, produced. The son resented the father's attitude and came to resent his own masculinity and that of other men. He became highly competitive with an urge to destroy the masculinity of others by outdoing them. A mother, who was anything but feminine, objected to the frills and fancy clothes her daughter liked to wear. The daughter later became a latent homosexual unable to accept her own feminity, and so remained unapproachable to men. In addition, she remained alienated from her own sex because of the coldness she had experienced from her mother in earlier years.

A third parental attitude influences the child's attitude toward other men and women; this is the attitude that parents have toward one another. Young boys frequently adopt an attitude toward their mother and toward other women which is identical with the attitude their father has toward their mother. Similarly, girls often adopt their mother's attitude toward their father and apply it to other men. In observing teenagers one is often struck with proof of this. For example, a teenage girl may construct within her own mind a picture of her father as a degenerate monster. The thing she does not realize is that all the pieces for that picture have been neatly cut out and handed to her by her mother. The daughter has simply fit them together to form the distorted image of her father which her mother has given her.

A boy tends to assimilate a picture of manhood from his father in his identification with him. A girl tends to paint a picture of womanhood along the lines outlined by her mother as the process of identification draws her into the mother's mold. If the father is too harsh, too severe with his son, the boy may turn from him and identify with the mother, thus developing feminine traits. If the process is severe enough, the youth may turn to homosexuality. If the father, on the other hand, is an extremely weak individual and the mother is the domineering, aggressive member of the marital pair, the son may again identify with the mother in an attempt to establish a strong aggressive personality more suited to his manhood.

There is also a maternal role in shaping a son's sexual identification. A woman who belittles her husband and turns to her young son for companionship and comfort places the son in a masculine role, but one which is most uncomfortable for him, since it carries the implication of an incestuous relationship with the mother. Such a son may flee from his masculinity and attempt to deny it by seeking refuge in homosexual adjustments.

A girl's attitude about her own sex and her orientation in a sexual role may be influenced in a similar way by paternal and maternal attitudes. Sexual identification is not used here in the limited sense of sexual activity, but in the broader sense of attitudes about one's own sex and one's relationship with other men and women.

Certainly, the problems of homosexuality do exist in the religious life. However, in communities of women it is not the active homosexual that causes the most frequent harm. It is rather the woman who is afraid of her own womanhood and denies it by her frigidity of temperament. She is not content to conceal her physical attributes in the garb of religion, but wishes also to bury her feminine attitudes under the guise of religion. She sets up walls around her heart that are bleaker than those around her convent. It is not woman's physical beauty that makes her God's fairest flower. It is the warmth of her love, the softness of her spirit, her sensitivity to hurt, to wrong, to sorrow. Why should God's own garden be full of shrinking violets? A religious must be alive and in her life must sublimate, not destroy, those qualities which on the natural plane would bring her to the grandeur of motherhood. She who denies these qualities brings an empty shell to the religious life instead of a rich, vibrant, vital human being.

One could not discuss the influence of family life on personality, and particularly on the development of attitudes toward our fellow man, without saying a word about prejudice. Family life is the cradle of prejudice, for it is here that children learn that "Negroes are dirty," that "Catholics are superstitious fools," that "Jews are money mad." Catholic families often have their own prejudices, and these are imparted to their children. A few of them might read like this: "Protestants aren't as good as we are;" "Public school children all do bad things;" "Priests and nuns are always right and know everything about anything." Such ideas in Catholic homes are certain to have their effect on the personality of the children coming from those homes.

Another area in which parents influence their child's attitude toward others is the all-important area of authority. Everyone remains subject to various sources of authority; the individual's response to that authority, his acceptance or rejection of it, is largely influenced by his early relationship to the authority of his parents. The manner in which parents use their God-given authority will deeply affect the child's attitudes toward other sources of authority. If parental authority is unjust it breeds resentment. If it is coercive it breeds resistance. If it is autocratic it breeds rebellion.

In this regard, there are two items of special interest: one is the use of punishment, the second is the acceptance of a child's anger.

An interesting insight into the personality of an individual is obtained by inquiring about the manner in which he was punished as a child and the reasons for being punished. Children have an almost innate sense of justice and fair play. If this sense of justice is wronged by parents who punish too severely or inappropriately, children will become hostile toward authority figures and be either weakly submissive to them and at the same time subtly rebellious, or they will rebel in defiant delinquency.

A thirteen year old girl who had repeatedly been unjustly punished by her parents was being interviewed because she refused to go to school. In a moment of candor and confidence, she described her absence from school as "quiet anger." This was her way of avenging herself against the injustice of her parents. Psychiatrists often see children of normal or superior intelligence who cannot seem to pass their schoolwork. Much of this behavior is "quiet anger." They reject personal responsibility as they rebel against parental authority.

There are obvious parallels between such behavior and that of some religious in the convent. There are varying responses on the part of Sisters to the authority of the superior. It is doubtful that there is one ideal response from a psychological point of view. Humble submission to the superior as the spokesman of God's will is the ideal on the supernatural plane. Most Sisters who remain struggling along in the purgative way cannot sublimate their feelings to such lofty ideals. They may intellectually accept the superior's word as God's will, but emotionally they may be rebellious and resentful. It is certainly true that they will be happier and healthier religious if they are somehow allowed to express their resentment, as long as they accept their assignment. At least one thing is certain: the most obvious place in which a Sister's relationship to her superior is going to be affected by early training in the home is in her attitude toward that superior's authority.

Another important factor in developing proper attitudes toward authority is parental acceptance of a child's anger. Many parents and, one might add, many religious superiors cannot tolerate an angry response from their subjects. This is another area interesting to explore with teenagers. Here is a typical response. "My parents are the only ones that are allowed to get angry in my house. If I am mad and go in my room and close the door, they come and open it." It is like telling a child that he's not allowed to get hungry; for anger is as natural a response to some real or imaginary hurt as hunger is to an empty stomach. To become angry is not unhealthy; children, as well as adults, must be allowed to be angry. However, there are mature and immature ways of showing anger. Children should be guided by parents in developing maturity in their reactions when they are angry.

An additional word should be said here about family relationships and their influence on personality. In a home where either or both parents have a distorted concept of their own sexuality, or use one or more of their children to further their own ends, there is the strong likelihood of frank favoritism and the concomitant possibility of jealousy among the children. When parents have a problem child, the circumstance is often one of favoritism. Parents are usually reluctant to admit favoritism, but will do so with some encouragement. Invariably, one of two situations will exist. Each parent has a child who is favored over the problem child, or the problem child is the favorite of one parent who, in turn, is hostile toward the other parent. The child gets caught in a no-man's land between the parents, with the father defending him and the mother attacking him, or vice versa.

Sibling rivalry created in the home can become a driving force which motivates the individual in his relationships with others outside the home. Fierce competitiveness, jealousy for one's peers, a highly critical and derogatory attitude toward others are the harvest that is reaped from the seeds of sibling jealousies. The presence of these attitudes in community life strike at the very core of fraternal charity, which is the psychological as well as the spiritual pole around which communal life must turn in order to function properly.

From a discussion of an individual's attitudes toward authority figures, it is natural to turn attention to a person's attitude toward the source of all authority, God. Ideally, rationally, supernaturally, one should see the authority of parents, of superiors, of civil authorities in the light of God's authority. Psychologically, the reverse is often true. One sees the authority of God, the fatherhood of God in the light of what one has experienced from authority figures here on earth.

Thus, the individual's concept of God may be strongly colored by his own image of his father, his mother, and other authority figures. The scrupulous person is, perhaps, the clearest example of such a relationship. Essentially, the scrupulous person cannot be impressed by the mercy of God, but sees only the severity of an avenging Deity who is determined to exact the most stringent penalty for every blemish upon one's soul. In the background of such a person there is frequently a parent who was strict, severe, demanding; one who weighed all in the balance and saw things as black or white, with no interspersed grays.

A priest patient had, in his youth, been stripped and beaten with a rope by his father until he bled. He was not only punished too severely, but frequently without cause. He was punished when anything went wrong, whether it was his sister's fault or the misdemeanor of some boy from the neighborhood. As a priest, he maintained his equilibrium sufficiently to impart the sacrament of forgiveness to others. Yet it was only a mechanical act because he had no feeling for forgiveness. How could he possibly believe in the mercy of God when his father, who gave him life, was so unmerciful? How could he believe in the justice of God when his father, who supposedly loved him, was so unjust?

Parents who love their children when they are wrong, but not because they are wrong, who do not estrange themselves from their erring sons and daughters, live the biblical story of the father of the Prodigal Son. Certainly Christ did not tell that story to extoll the life of the Prodigal, but to exemplify the attitude of a merciful and loving father. How, then, can parents or relatives be asked to ostracize one of the family who may be illegitimately pregnant, or married outside the Church, or living a scandalous life?

Finally, there is a fourth set of attitudes which is necessary for a mature personality: the attitudes one has toward the task of living, toward one's personal responsibilities. This personality factor is also greatly influenced by the attitude of parents in the home. Family life is a cooperative venture, or at least it should be. The sooner each member of the family becomes part of the group by accepting some of the chores that are always present in the home, the sooner each member will feel that he truly belongs to this family unit and that he shares the responsibility of keeping it going. Sharing the task of family living helps bring family members closer together and teaches them to engage in cooperative effort. It is often quoted that the family which prays together stays together. One might add that the family which plays together learns to enjoy one another's company, and the family which works together learns respect for one another. There are obvious applications of this concept in community living.

The best way for a child to learn the lesson of responsibility is to have some specific duties to perform around the home. Some parents teach their children everything except the lesson of work. They teach them the social graces for the purpose of getting ahead, not for the purpose of getting along. They teach them to enjoy the good things in life without teaching how to earn them. Or they pay their children for everything they do, and so teach them that work is valued only through its monetary reward. Children should learn to work because work is part of life. They must learn to respect work because work is respectable. They must learn to accept work because work brings some of life's greatest satisfactions.

Consideration has been given to some specific ways in which family life, particularly parental attitudes, can influence the personality of the developing child. These are but samples of such influence. There are many factors, many relationships, many subtleties which are involved. Family influence on personality is so great that if one were given insight into the many forces operating within a home and upon a given individual, one could predict fairly accurately what sort of personality that individual would have in later years.

If communities wish to understand those who approach their doors for admission to the religious life, or those who live within the quiet walls and the sacred vows of their convents, let them look to the parents who gave them life. Consider the cradle from which they came, and attend to the lengthy shadow of the homes which follow and rest upon them, no matter how brilliantly their own sun may shine.

CHAPTER III

SELF IMAGE AND SELF ACCEPTANCE

It is the fate of each human being to somehow bear the burden of himself. Some carry it easily because they fail to recognize it as a burden. Others carry it without concern because they really do not carry it at all, but only fall beneath its pressure and do not try to rise again. But the one inescapable burden of the religious life is the burden of self. For this life makes one aware of self, forces one to look behind and see the ported pack of past experiences. This life metes out in measured judgments verdicts concerned with self along a scale that stretches to eternity.

Self image is important to everyone. It is the vortex around which the currents of emotional life must move, it is the pole around which the winds of life experiences must center. What one thinks about oneself as a human being is really the pivot from which one forms opinions about others and about life itself.

For the person in religion this self-concept is doubly important. The religious must first decide who she is as a human being, and secondly she must decide who she is as a religious. But this latter concept is based so directly and completely on the former that it is almost impossible for the religious to have a favorable concept of herself as a Sister if she does not have a good concept of herself as a human being.

Without too much strain, it is possible for a woman to think of herself as a good school teacher but a bad person. The world would accept the fact that a woman of ill repute might at the same time be a very capable teacher. A woman could conceive of herself as a good nurse, a competent stenographer, even a good housewife and an acceptable mother and at the same time consider herself to be a person of little personal worth. The conflict would not be too severe. The result might be a rather unsettled nurse, a somewhat anxious stenographer, a slightly neurotic wife and mother; but the two different value judgments about herself would possibly not make life unbearable for her. Such is obviously not the case for the religious, and it is precisely on this point that many religious get into difficulty with themselves, with their superiors, and with their vocation.

The religious who has a poor opinion of herself as a human being can hardly see herself as a good religious. If she is not worthwhile as a human being, if she has no sense of personal worth, how then can she be a good religious? But being a good religious is something which is constantly held up to her, not just as an ideal but as a practical solution to fulfilling her chosen state in life and thus ultimately saving her own soul. It is obvious that the conflict for the religious cannot help but be a severe one, and may easily come to be an intolerable one. She is expected to be worthy to be the bride of Christ, but she sees herself as worthless.

On the spiritual level no one is worthy to approach Christ, but on the natural level don't we say that we should bring our gifts, our talents, all that is best in us and give it to God? This poor wretch finds no good in herself and so approaches the wedding feast without a wedding garment. It is difficult and perhaps impossible to be comfortable in such a situation. This is the discomfort of not belonging – one of the most intolerable anxieties that can trouble human beings.

If there are criteria for accepting candidates for religious communities, women who have a sense of personal dignity should be considered first. They are already one step toward the dignity of being a religious. One of the core concepts of the Catholic faith is the dignity of every human being because he is a human being, not because he is black or white, intelligent or feeble-minded, handsome or misshapen and ugly – but simply because he is a human being with a soul which will exist eternally and for which Christ died. This is something each of us learned from the catechism long ago. Yet many Catholics and some religious cannot seem to accept it in practice. It has no meaning in their lives. They somehow see the Negro without that dignity, the sinner without that worth, the poor and ignorant without that value. Perhaps it is because they see themselves without dignity. Perhaps they never learned the lesson of their own personal worth. So if one seeks religious who will see the worth of other human beings and thereby breathe life into the sterile form of distant dogma, it is important to choose those who respect themselves and who expect others to respect them.

This sense of personal worth should be fostered in the novitiate. If novices are treated as women of dignity, if they are respected because they are human beings and not because they are novices, their sense of personal worth will grow.

There is a narrow but careful distinction that should be emphasized in this regard. Note that the statement was made that they should be respected because they are human beings, because they are individuals, and not because they are novices, not because they are young women who desire to dedicate themselves to God. It is important for the religious to be trained in the knowledge – and after training to remember the fact – that she is worthwhile first and foremost because she is a human being and not because she is a Sister and living a life of dedicated virginity. It is important for several reasons. First of all, because it is true. Secondly, it makes the possibility of leaving the convent a tolerable consideration. The Sister who associates her basic worth with her role as a religious would be totally shattered, utterly destroyed psychologically, by leaving the convent, so cannot bring herself to consider such a decision. It is not that the religious life needs her, but that she needs it in order to survive emotionally. Her decision to remain may consequently lack free choice. Thirdly, it gives her a better perspective on her later failures in the life of religion. It must be assumed that most of those who enter the religious life are really not going to turn out to be perfect.

The self-concept of being worthwhile must not be allowed to depend on something which is accidental. It cannot depend on what one does or does not do. If it depends on what one does, then there is an inevitable conclusion to be drawn when the time comes that she happens not to do what has previously made her feel worthwhile. She simply loses her personal dignity. Just like that! So this sense of worth should not be imparted to a novice *because* she is a novice. This is somewhat akin to the bitter pill that many Negroes must swallow these days when they meet with respect just because they are Negroes. The wheel of fortune came up on black and they can now cash in their color for the coin of courtesy. They *should* be respected because they are human beings worthy of respect and not because they are dark-skinned.

Perhaps our Protestant brothers feel the same way at times as a result of the ecumenical movement. It is now fashionable to respect them, to be interested in them and in what they think and feel. Do we respect them because they are Protestants or because they are creatures of dignity and individual worth? If it is the latter, then what has been going on for the past few centuries? They must in some instances believe it is the former, and in some instances they may be right.

There is a peculiar danger in giving novices a sense of dignity based on their dedication to religion. Such an atmosphere may nourish the wrong plants, for weeds grow as quickly as flowers in surface soil that receives daily watering. It is exactly those young women who lack a sense of personal worth who would be most impressed by such an environment and succumb to the seduction of its psychological promise. They are searching for a feeling of worth and attempt to find it in pleasing others or in some activity in which they engage. Parenthetically, it should be noted that they never find it in this manner, because there is always the danger that those who are pleased today may tomorrow be displeased, or the activity which can be performed today may tomorrow be obviated by change of circumstances. If a young woman's sense of worth comes from being a good novice, she must cling in desperation to her façade of obedience and piety, lest she let slip from her grasp that which she has never really held securely and then meet again in despair the void that is left to her.

Such an environment – one which bases personal worth on some accident of behavior or of decision in the novitiate and for that matter in the community itself – may also turn away others who have a wholesome concept of self. These Sisters desire to be respected for themselves, and they may in fact demand to be so respected. If pseudo-spiritual sentimentality prevents it, they may decide that their needs can better be satisfied elsewhere. And quite properly so! For if an individual has this healthy sense of pride and enters a community that would root out all self-expression and individuality, she is either doomed to unhappiness or elevated to high virtue; and the latter comes not quickly nor often. This healthy sense of pride is perhaps not different from humility. Indeed it sounds as accurate to call it by the latter name.

Before going on to consider what happens to the religious and her self-image, it might be well to give some consideration to the origin of the self concept. How do we arrive at this opinion about ourselves? It is learned like everything else that we learn and the teaching comes either directly through the words and admonitions of others or indirectly through the attitudes of others, which can be communicated by frank or subtle reactions on their part. Where does the child learn his concept of God? Where does he learn his concept of what other human beings are like? Where does the child learn his prejudices? Where does he learn to respect or not to respect authority? All of these are learned from those adults who are psychologically important to him. They hold up the mirror in which he sees himself reflected in the attitudes they have toward him. His parents are of first importance here, but other relatives, neighbors, and teachers (they should never be forgotten) are also very important. How do these go about teaching him a sense of personal worth, a healthy self concept? Fundamentally, it depends on how they treat him, on how they regard him. If the child is seen as an individual with a dignity all his own, a person who has rights, who has attitudes, who has his own needs, who has desires, who has feelings of love, of anger, of resentment, who has his own thoughts – if all of this happens in the minds of adults, then it is likely to be transmitted to the mind of the child and he will see himself in the same way. The foundation of this process is to respect the child for what he is and not for what he does, and by word – but even more important, by action – to carefully distinguish between the two. The child who is rejected, totally disapproved of because he has done something naughty, loses his sense of personal worth. His self concept at that time shares his parents' attitude that he is just bad, that he is totally bad. It is important to remember that this all takes place when the child is completely defenseless, when his need for parental acceptance and approval is as important to him psychologically as food and shelter are to him physically.

There are many ways in which this lack of fundamental worth can be communicated to the child, and there are many areas in which adults can decrease the child to nothingness. Some parents start early. They take it as a personal affront when their child is not the first in the entire neighborhood to be toilet trained, to tie his own shoes, to eat with a spoon. This appears to them to be a direct attack upon their own integrity as parents. They show in various ways their disapprobation of the child. There is an entire gamut which the child must survive to please such parents, and sooner or later, being somewhat less than perfect, he fails. Then he is condemned, no matter how many times he has succeeded before, no matter how many challenges he has met, no matter how many times he has given his all to satisfy the ego of his parents.

Parents compete with other parents in many unconscious ways through their children. They attempt to realize their own unfulfilled desires through their children. Certainly all parents do not do these things, but many do and it is their children who grow in the knowledge that they are not of value intrinsically but only accidentally through what they can produce to please their parents. This may sound exaggerated, but there are some examples from everyday life which may make it sound a bit more realistic. One set of parents wants their child to be the most intelligent in the class. It is not too unusual that parents want to know the I.Q. of their child; often this is not so they can help their child set realistic goals for himself, but so they can boast about it if the I.Q. is high. If it isn't high, they usually discuss at length the limitations of psychological testing, but there is also some secret disapproval of their less-than-perfect child. Another child must be the best dressed in the school or the most washed in the neighborhood. Another must be a good athlete, another popular, another talented of voice or of limb in order to please some expectant mother – twice expectant because she once gave physical birth to a separate human being, and now wants to destroy the separateness of the child and cause him to be psychologically reborn into her own image and likeness. Children sometimes die *in utero* because they are strangled by the umbilical cord which gets wrapped around their neck. Children sometimes die psychologically because the umbilical cord of parental expectation wraps itself around them and strangles them.

The human spirit rebels at slavery, at oppression, at loss of personal freedom; but this form of slavery, this type of personal destruction is done under the guise of what is best for the child and frequently is quasi-spiritualized by sprinkling it with pious prattle about the fourth commandment. "Honor your father and mother" does *not* mean being bright, popular, industrious, athletic, clean, etc., because father and mother want it so.

Teachers can be as guilty as parents when they reject a child as a person because he is mischievous, or because he doesn't work up to his capacity, or, to be honest, because he doesn't meet their expectations. The heart of the matter rests in that remark – the child is rejected as a person because he does not meet the expectations of some important adult. What happens is that the adult puts a price tag on the child which is a reflection solely of his behavior. When he behaves as desired by the shopkeeper his price tag goes up; when he behaves otherwise his price tag goes down. He never learns that he has another value which is his priceless human soul. This soul gives him the power to think, to reason, to love, to weep, to fall and rise again; and his value is not determined by whether or not he thinks or weeps, but by the fact that he can do such things – in short because he is human.

Perhaps now it is more obvious why the young religious, and for that matter the old religious, with a poor self image must have such a struggle with the religious life. She has not the security of recognizing her own personal dignity. She must look for it in things she does. But her life calls for perfection. It is true we are all called to perfection. But the life of the religious is a louder trumpet than most of us hear. She cannot escape its call for she hears it in her spiritual exercises, she knows its notes through her daily examen, she recognizes the theme of its music reflected in her garb, her associates, in all that she does. There are religious who try to solve the conflict thus created by attempting to deaden the trumpet's constant call. They skip their spiritual exercises, they stop saying the office, their prayers, they avoid their fellow religious, they stay away from recreation – for all these things remind them of the life they find themselves unable to fulfill in a way sufficient to give them the feeling of personal worth which they crave. This course provides no respite. It is only a temporary plateau of peace. They remain haunted by the need for the self esteem they destroy daily. They struggle with their vocation and may leave the convent. They struggle with their own mind and it may lose its equilibrium. Whichever way they turn they are unhappy souls who are the victims of their own past life. Their future holds little promise of fulfillment because an emptiness has become part of their personality.

Religious with this problem are difficult to treat in psychotherapy, as are lay people who have the same problem. The goal of therapy is to give them now what they never had as children. The therapist must accept them and respect them no matter what they are, even though he might not approve of what they do. They often tax this relationship severely by doing things which make it difficult for them to be accepted and loved. Careful distinction must be maintained between their excellence as human beings and the impropriety of their behavior. They have been deprived in childhood of a basic requirement for their psychological growth. They are like the person who has been starved for months or years and who eats ravenously when food is available, sometimes so greedily that he makes himself ill. They have been deprived of the feeling of personal dignity. They continue to crave it and know only one way to attempt to attain it. They anxiously pursue perfection in order to obtain from others the praise they need to establish their own worth now. They have considerable difficulty, therefore, accepting that which is less than perfect within themselves. Their imperfections make them anxious and become intolerable to their self image. Therapy must attempt to make them comfortable in their own imperfections. They must learn to accept themselves and be secure the way they are before they can ever hope to effect a change in themselves.

Religious sometimes get side-tracked in their own best efforts by their inability to accept themselves. Because of the intensity of their spiritual life, or perhaps it would be better to say because of the frequency and purpose of their spiritual exercises, they sometimes focus on their imperfections and lose perspective on themselves. Self-evaluation and introspection are often hazardous processes. People sometimes gaze so lengthily (perhaps lovingly) in the mirror of self examination that they fail to see the world around them. They become self absorbed, even though the focus of that absorption is some imperfection. They say to themselves, "Someday, when I rid myself of this particular vice, then I shall do all the good that I would like to do. Someday, when I am no longer such and such a person, then I shall do so and so." The world would make little progress if it had to wait for people to rid themselves of vices before they got under way to accomplish something.

Mental patients must sometimes learn to use pigeon-holes. These can be useful devices for most people at times. A pigeon-hole is a mental tool used to wall off one thing by placing it in a little compartment within the mind, which takes on the characteristics of a pigeon-hole desk. This is done in order to keep this object or this experience or this habit of behavior from contaminating the rest of one's life and the rest of one's mind. The individual rather deliberately refuses to consider something. He refuses to see his entire life under the aura of this imperfection or sin. Then he lives his life as if this problem didn't exist, rather than using the problem as an excuse for not accomplishing anything else positive in life. The mind is an intricate mechanism and sometimes plays the worst tricks on the best of us. When an imperfection serves as a block to doing some other worthwhile things, there may be an interesting bit of self-deceit in this. The imperfection or habit of sin may in fact be exactly what was suggested before, i.e., an excuse for not taking responsibility for some positive behavior in other areas. When such a situation occurs, one of the best ways to overcome the imperfection is to behave as if it didn't exist. When these responsibilities are accepted in other areas, the reason for the imperfection may be removed automatically.

The religious life poses its own particular threat to the individual's self-concept. In such a life there is the danger that role may be confused with true identity and the former replace the latter. In different ways the religious life seeks to disguise the identity of the person and to conceal the uniqueness of the personality under the cloak of community conformity, much as the special appearance of the person is concealed under the common uniform of the habit. Such a life must truly endanger the self concept for it tends to hide the self from view and from expression. This situation is peculiar to the religious, for it is only the religious who can never escape from this all-encompassing role. A school teacher on her summer vacation can forget completely that she is a school teacher, and many of them do. An office girl can leave the anonymity of her office job for another anonymity of her own choosing. Even a housewife can get away from being a housewife for a while and see herself as distinct from this role which she has assumed. In fact, psychiatrists often recommend to the bored housewife or the harassed mother that she get out of the home and assume some other role in life.

Such a change is not open to the religious. She is and remains a religious twenty-four hours a day, 365 days of the year. She apparently ceases to be anything other than a religious. Is this a healthy situation? Sister is something more than a religious. She is first of all a person. She should not lose that notion of herself in the religious life. If she does, she may lose herself and suffer the disintegration of personality which follows from such a loss, or she may lose her vocation because she refuses to tolerate that loss of identity. It is not easy to counteract this loss of identity in the convent. A priest can take off his distinctive garb and become a golfer, a vacationer, an average citizen, etc. Such a change is usually not available to Sister. Her sense of identity might be partially maintained by a feeling of freedom to be herself at least within the confines of her convent walls. There are religious today who are doing very important work outside their own communities, work which is recognized by both the Catholic and secular press. However, some of these same Sisters are not allowed to talk about their work within their own communities because there are some in the community who do not believe they should be involved in it. Chesterton commented on a man's home being the one place where he is really free to be an individual. How frustrated a religious must feel if she cannot relax and communicate freely with others within her own convent which is now her home!

There are religious who are so much religious that they almost cease to be human beings; in fact, they sometimes seem a little less than human. These may be contrasted with the vibrant, vital, sparkling people in the convent that one never forgets because they are, first of all, people and, secondly, very wonderful Sisters. Patients often ask psychiatrists who may be encouraging them to get angry, to love, to express themselves, "*How* should I get angry, *how* should I love someone, *how* should I express myself?" They are frequently disturbed when the psychiatrist tells them that he doesn't really know how they should do these things because they must do them in their own individual way. By the same token, it is impossible to tell people *how* to be good religious. They can be given the cold rules, the hard lines, the sharp principles. How each one of them lives this life can only be settled in terms of each one's own personality, each one's own abilities and deficiencies, each one's own unique approach to living and to living as a religious. Living in the close quarters of convent life makes a certain uniformity essential for reasonable order. However, the superior who fosters the independence of individual thought, who respects the variety of individual differences will find her charges a more contented group than if this were not so.

The woman in religious life must settle many questions in her own mind. She must answer for herself what it means theoretically to live the religious life, what it means theoretically to be a Sister, what it means theoretically to be a member of this community. Then she must answer each of these questions again in a *practical* way. But before she can begin to understand these questions she must also ask herself another question. This first question she must consider and resolve and never forget is: what it means to be a person, a human being, an individual.

There is a peculiar psychology involved in a certain number of those who defect from religious life. They have always been model religious, perfect examples for everyone else. They live this way because they prove their own worth by being diligent in perfection and by denying their own imperfections, their own limitations. They cannot tolerate the weakness, indeed at times the wickedness, of their own humanity. They conceal it from others. They even conceal it from themselves. Then one day their humanity breaks through the defense they have built around it. The entire structure crumbles because it was built too rigidly, without the elasticity necessary to support stress. They flee the religious life because they cannot face themselves as imperfect religious. Perhaps the psychology of some intellectual political defectors is similar. They deny the imperfections of their own government because their own emotional needs require it to be perfect. Suddenly some incident forces them finally to acknowledge its flaws and, unable to tolerate this blemished image, they flee to some new visionary allegiance.

The burden of self which the religious bears is the burden of her own imperfections in a life which calls for perfection, the burden of sin in a life which is replete with self examination, the burden of her past in a new life where she seems to become another person. Some will bear this burden well, perhaps because it weighs on them less heavily, or perhaps because they are less sensitive to what they carry. For those who carry it with discomfort and distaste, for those whom it bites as it bends, whom it tears as it torments, the words of Louis Beirnaert seem particularly appropriate: "There are the saints whose psychic structures are deformed and difficult, the company of the anguished, aggressive and sensual, all those who bear an insupportable weight of determinism; the failures in whose heart there will always be a 'viper's tangle,' the unfortunate, because they are born with a 'harelip.' There are those who will never charm the birds or caress the wolf of Gubbio; those who fall, and will fall again; those who will weep to the end, not because they have knocked too loudly at a door, but because they have committed again this sin – sordid, unmentionable. There is the immense throng of those in whom sanctity will never shine in their psychic structure here below, who will never lift themselves up till the last day to be resplendent *in perpetuas aeternitates.* These are saints without the name."

It is safe to assume that most of the saints who live in convents are among the saints who shall never be named.

CHAPTER IV

THE PSYCHOLOGY OF COMMUNITY

Soldiers die in Viet Nam, and we watch the event on television with little more emotion than we might watch a re-run of "All Quiet on the Western Front." Citizens die in the racial violence of Detroit and, as we scan the photographs of death on the front pages of our newspapers, we hurry on to the comic page because of our concern with the death of one of Rex Morgan's patients. Children die of hunger in American slums, and their dying is not as noteworthy as the death of an animal in the local zoo. Rats take over human housing in the ghettos, and we are amused by the phantasy problems of Snoopy and the Red Baron.

There are some touchstones of human psychology in such a commentary, just as there is some insult to individual integrity in such realities. We prefer not to recognize that these reactions are to some extent true of all of us. It is a strange and startling phenomenon that we can weep and be sad so inconsistently, at times so inappropriately, and at times so inadequately.

The world in which the individual lives is largely structured within his own mind. He weeps for things that make him sad, and the objective tragedies of our times may fail to touch him. He finds humor in a situation that contains none of the characteristics of levity, but because it has some special meaning for him. His joy may come from the shouts of little children because they are his children, while at the same moment their noise may be most annoying to others.

In order to establish some foundation for the psychology of community, it is important to understand that the community in which an individual lives is largely structured by the past memories, present needs, and persistent anxieties that live within the individual. The term, community, does not define a precise, generally accepted body of people. One person's community may include the soldiers of Viet Nam, the victims and/or the perpetrators of riot, hungry children, those in the ghettos. Another may be more involved in the community of movie characters or comic strips. Any one of these attitudes may be a defense against the possibility of becoming involved more directly in a real community.

To consider the psychology of community living with any clarity, there must be some understanding of what is referred to as community. The rules of relating to a community which is a figment of one's own imagination are quite different than the rules of relating to the reality of other people. The schizophrenic may establish very pleasant relationships with the people-like productions of his own delusions. The unconventional pet lover may establish workable relationships with a quasi-community of cats or dogs. It is not too difficult to relate to the contents of a particular delusion or to the pets of a particular household, both of which can be manipulated to match particular needs and desires. We sense, however, that this is not community living, because it does not involve flesh and blood people.

There are strong voices claiming that we must have a sense of community which includes those dying in Viet Nam, those who starve daily and die slowly, those who are poor, oppressed, or objects of discrimination. Can these truly be part of our community if we are not involved in some meaningful and personal relationship with them? Or is this community of distant fact no more realistic than that of immediate fiction? Can the true life story of Pvt. John Smith in Viet Nam be more lifelike than the latest adventures of Agent 007?

True community living must involve direct and meaningful contact between the individual and the group. It must be a reciprocal relationship whereby the individual makes some significant contact with the community, and the latter in turn responds to him. In order for this to happen, the community must have some structure and some boundaries, some rather concrete definition. The community which is nebulous because it is not known, which is vague because its membership expands endlessly, cannot respond in a meaningful way to the individual.

The individual and the community are sometimes considered antithetical to one another. One must choose to live as a true communist or one must be a hermit. One must follow the party line, the group philosophy, the Jones' lead, or one must be a rugged individualist and stand alone. The ideal of community living is to maintain some middle stand between these two extremes. The individual must be permitted, even encouraged, to remain an individual in his community contacts, but he must give something of himself in his belonging to the group.

It is proper and it is psychologically necessary for the individual to maintain his individuality. If he has successfully weathered the turmoil of teen years he has achieved a level of maturity which gives him some recognition of his uniqueness and separateness as an individual. A sense of identity and a sense of worth are ingredients of his individuality. Before a person can relate in the healthiest manner to a community, he must have achieved this level of maturity. As a result of this individuality, the person experiences freedom, self-determination. This aspect of the psychology of community living is important to keep in mind, for it is often forgotten by those who concentrate on community relationships. The person who has not achieved some satisfactory level of maturity will have particular difficulties in attempting group interaction. He will expect to find an identity which community cannot give him. He will be unable to relinquish freedom which he has not yet achieved and will expect the community to give him guidance because he lacks self-determination.

Different people define community differently because they emphasize different characteristics of its structure. Community involves joining with others in a psychological manner and sharing with those others some common purposes and participating in some common actions to achieve those purposes. The phrase "joining with others in a psychological manner" implies that there is a certain attitude present on the part of the members. Their psychological attitude, their interest is far more important than their physical presence. The term "some common purposes" suggests that this group need not have all their purposes in common, only some of them. Similarly, the term "some common actions" implies that the group need not act as a unit in every way or on every matter, but only on some.

It would seem essential to this concept of community to posit that these common purposes must extend beyond those of the individual and not be simply synonymous with the goals of a single person. The individual who belongs to a community, therefore, just to achieve his own goals without any genuine concern for the goals of the community is not in fact a psychological member of that community, although he and the community may both mistakenly believe him to be.

Another characteristic of community that is important is that its limits be reasonably well defined. The more elusive the boundaries are, the more the individual is likely to lose himself, to lose his identity, in an attempt to relate to it, and the less likelihood there is of a meaningful response from the community. Perhaps the most dangerous form of false community is that which has enough substance to hold the individual but not enough solidarity to offer him any significant response.

The psychology of healthy community living requires on the part of the individual the achievement of his own identity and sense of individuality prior to his involvement with the group. In addition, this fact of his individuality must be preserved while he is engaged in interaction with the community. He must not be consumed in the group process nor in the community need. His personal integrity must be preserved.

If the person has not matured to the point where he has achieved the stable position of his own individuality, he cannot become a firm and effective member of the community. As a corollary, if the community in some way threatens his individuality, he will cease to be a beneficial member of the group. Abandonment of group allegiance may be the only method of preserving his own individuality.

The psychology of defection from the religious life (as well as political defections) frequently involves such a choice. This does not imply that religion or the Church as such threatens one's individuality, but undoubtedly the immediate community structure under which a person lives does in some instances destroy one's individuality. One of the other principal psychological causes of defection is the situation in which the person is not sufficiently mature to enter into the interchanges that are demanded in the structured community of the religious life. The problem in this case is not in the community but in the immaturity of the individual.

As long as the individual can maintain his sense of identity and individuality, the community becomes one of his most productive and creative relationships. It is only in an exchange with others that the person can attain the development of his fullest potential. The community, whether it be within the home, within the church, within the profession or place of work, within the neighborhood or club, becomes both the stimulus for and the recipient of the individual's energy, imagination and creativity. It is in this sense that the individual needs the community, for he is indeed limited without it.

There is some paradox, however. The individual is limited in the expression of himself without the group, but he is also limited in his self-expression when he is within the group. Everyone has limitations, but the ability to recognize one's limitations is itself limited. Meaningful contact with the community provides the individual with a kind of mirroring experience. Self knowledge is difficult to arrive at within the little workshop of one's own mind. There is need for a sounding board, a feed-back. Community contacts serve this purpose, for they give us the opportunity to look at ourselves in the looking glass called "others."

The person who refrains from community living or withdraws from social interaction is somewhat like the person who is placed in an experimental situation of sensory deprivation. When a person is maintained in an environment which is devoid of sensory stimulation, he frequently begins to produce his own apparent sensory impressions, although in fact these are hallucinatory. In a similar way, the person who remains aloof from community contacts has no resounding media which stimulate his continuing adjustment. He is left free, in a sense, to evaluate his own behavior, his own attitudes, without reference to external criteria. Considerable reference is made, in a pejorative manner toward psychiatry, to the fact that many emotionally disturbed persons recover without the aid of professional attention. This is unquestionably true. One of the processes whereby they recover is the corrective life experience that results from contacts with others. The person who is isolated has no one to educate him about himself.

Some may try to substitute relationships with individuals for group relationships. Such an arrangement is almost as fallible as one's own evaluation of self. The group has a broader base from which to evaluate the individual, for the dissimilar views of its members give it a certain objectivity. The individual relationship can be a kind of defense against community involvement that is used by some who are threatened by the objectivity of the latter. Every community, every movement, every cause has this kind of member. He relates singly to one or several but has no concept of the group as a whole. Perhaps some of the movements within the church to emphasize community are a reaction to the situation in which the "favored few" are separately engulfed in the psychological embrace of individual religious, and the many are left on the periphery of a community which does not seem to contain them.

One must stand on tiptoe and look over the high brim of self to the needs of others if one is to participate in community. Such participation involves more than just looking at the needs of others. It involves an emotional understanding of those needs and this leads to a relevant contact with those who have need.

One might ask, "What is the basic psychological relationship of the members within a community?" It must be more than an intellectual appreciation of one another, of the needs and common goals. It cannot be expected to contain the ardor of personal love, but it is a kind of caring for these others, a caring that reaches beyond the boundary of self and combines in common force to benefit all.

Some moderns in a rather desperate search for community – desperate because their own identity is erroneously involved – rush to a depth of relationship which community structure will not support. They speak of dialogue, of commitment, of the I and the Thou, of many things for which they hunger. They do not realize that all their needs cannot be satiated by community living. They tax the bonds of communality because their demands threaten to topple the true values of community relationships. Need for personal love cannot be satisfied in community living. The intimate, direct relationship of personal love cannot be diffused to an entire community and remain intact. An attempt to elicit community response to such a personal need will likely terminate in utter frustration with the community experience. Or it may end in a kind of self-deception which permits a personal relationship to be disguised as a common cause. The stable and well-integrated person must recognize these four areas: first, his separate self; second, his intimate, personal, individual relationship in sincere love; third, his caring concerns for those with whom he joins himself in community; and fourth, his broader interest in social needs.

In order to explain and to expand some of this concept regarding communities it might be of value to consider some kinds of community structure which exist but which fall short of producing a healthy interaction with individuals or for individuals. Reference has already been made to some of these communities.

There is the fantasy community which exists in the mind of the individual. The extreme example is the fictitiously populated world of the schizophrenic. The person who is psychologically engrossed in the fantasy world of his own daydreams shares the same kind of orientation. The pet lover who abandons human company by substitution of animals eccentrically displays the same pattern. The most acceptable and most popular fantasy communities are those which include all of mankind, or all the members of one race, or all the oppressed. These are not communities in reality but become so only in the imagination of those who need to relate to them in some way. That we have a common brotherhood of all people, that we have an obligation to the oppressed, is certainly true. However, these do not qualify as communities, if one attempts to group all the poor together, all the oppressed together, etc. There can be no interaction between the individual and any of these groups; there can be no definite participation in purposes and means. Those who seek the anonymity of such participation may need to go back to learn the true lesson of community living. As one must achieve a healthy degree of individuality before progressing to the stage of community, so one must achieve an ability to interact on a true community level before progressing to the broader fields of social causes. Without learning the techniques of each successive step, one runs the risk of ruining one's own healthy productivity and one is likely, unwittingly, to sabotage the goals of the group and the aims of society.

A second kind of community is the comfortable one. It has as its purpose the comfort of its members, and this comfort surpasses any higher goals. It is usually a small community because it cannot tolerate the discomfort of disparity. The best example is the snob club whether it exists on the college campus, at the country club, or in the religious house. One of the means its members use to achieve their own psychological comfort is to exhibit a certain disdain for those who do not agree with them. They can hardly be called prejudiced since little judgment, even faulty judgment, is involved. They react to others as automatically as one reacts to a bad odor. Occasionally they absorb one or two members who disagree with their opinionated attitudes. The rebel member somehow increases the group self-complacency, perhaps by proving they are really not like others. Measured by the characteristics of community, this is a false community because it does not have goals which are beyond those of its individual members. The snob element often exists as a group within a larger community and often bases its imaginary excellence on the purity of its adherence to a cause, whether that cause be the liturgical movement, the problem of integration, or the reform of government. Beneath the disguise they are still repelled by the stench of humanity, themselves excepted.

A third kind of community is the disintegrating community. The cause of disintegration is twofold. First, individual members attempt to solve their problems of maturity through the group process. They look to the group to give them an identity which they do not possess. As a result they weaken group cohesiveness. Secondly, individual members detract from group needs by segmenting off other persons in an effort to have their own needs met. Group goals become subservient to individual goals. The best example of this kind of disintegrating community is unfortunately those religious communities whose members have not progressed to a psychological status adequate for community living. In the past they have been bound together by a set of rules which placed them in contiguity to one another but not in community with one another. As the rules which supported an artificial structure are loosened, the psychological maturity necessary for common living is found wanting. The clamor to satisfy one's own needs mutes the weakened cry for communality.

The fourth kind of community is the loosely structured one. There are no common goals, no mutually shared interests, but only the shadow of sodality. There is more of a clinging together than a banding together. Whatever they share in common is itself commonplace. This kind of community appears to have structure, but has little solidarity. It has sufficient structure to attract those who seek self identity in some common experience. It does not have sufficient solidarity to provide a reflection of self back to the individual. Joining such a community is like pushing one's arm into quicksand to find the bottom, or attempting to see one's own reflection in a cloud. There is not adequate substance to serve as end point to the individual's behavior.

The most appropriate example of such a community is that of the "hippies." They seek self in the uncertainty of others who are similarly confused. The group has no true identity, yet members individually seek some personal identity through the group. They shun the rest of society, and thereby avoid the corrective experience which other groups might provide for them. There is no absolute against which they can test and possibly transform their own attitudes and ideas. They are living in an emotional vacuum which they attempt to fill with drug-induced dreams. Their love is as unreal as their hate because they are unrelated to a community which they can neither love nor hate. The hostility of their behavior escapes them because they are not in contact with the community toward which their behavior is hostile. Their expressions of love are without effect because they are not in contact with anyone to love. They appear to be in anguish over the deceptions of the "straight world," but their greatest deception is their self-deception in not recognizing the anguish of their true loneliness, for indeed they are without community.

There is good reason to maintain a firm structure in a community because it allows for interrelationships between the individual members and the group. There is possibly something very deleterious to this relationship in the presently changing patterns within the church. It is not that change should not occur, but it is well to remember that during the span of change lines of structure are blurred. The individual finds affiliations obscured and alliances overburdened. The community which too quickly changes its inner formation will too readily leave behind some of its members. The goals of the group must not be retarded by those who are opposed to change. By the same token, those goals must not be changed by those who are in other ways opposed to the group. Are the *avant-gardes* greater champions of the community than the reactionaries? Not necessarily! Because the *avant-gardes* define their goals as goals toward which the group should strive, they avoid any designation of being oppositional. It is then so simple to label the conservatives as the oppositionists.

A fifth kind of community is the rigid one. This group has common goals and strict regulations to attain them. They are usually more absorbed in the regulations, however, than they are in the goals. They reject diversity of opinion within the community, and they condemn diversity of opinion outside their own group. They allow the individual little freedom in his relationship with the group. There is a kind of all-or-none attitude which is a basic premise of members. This attitude so predominates their thinking that others are not really allowed the freedom of not belonging to their community, even though they may not be permitted to join. The groups who fight various forms of prejudice are often founded on this premise. Everyone must join, everyone must believe. But, of course, if you do not agree with them you cannot join, even though you must. They are opposed to all forms of prejudice except their own form, which is to be prejudiced against the prejudiced. The group which fights for racial integration can be bitterly prejudiced against the segregationists. Groups which move into the area of inner city problems can become fanatically intolerant of suburban dwellers. Liturgists can become at least mildly opposed to groups which still want to sing some of the old hymns. There is nothing quite as righteous or as subtle as the prejudice of those who oppose prejudice.

There are other examples of such communities. Successful people are likely to join in some common activity or interest and have little tolerance for the unsuccessful members of society. Unfortunately, success is usually measured by the accumulation of wealth or fame, and not by true charity toward others. Education can develop a sort of elite community which has no patience with its absence in others, thereby proving that it is not synonymous with wisdom.

The comfortable community was mentioned above. There is another kind of community, the uncomfortable one. Participation in a group, if it is genuine, requires a great deal of those who participate, and perhaps more of some than of others. Man is undoubtedly a social animal, but the ease of his communal endeavor may vary greatly depending on the individual and upon the group to which he belongs. Because of inborn temperamental differences and because of early learning experiences, individuals differ in the readiness with which they form communal ties. The uncomfortable community contains a number of individuals who are not yet adjusted to the closeness of group companionship. Community living may be overwhelming to certain members and tend to keep them in peripheral positions. There are various discomforts that individuals may experience in relating to the group. Whether they are of real or imaginary origin is of little consequence.

Some of the new movements within the church, and perhaps certain aspects of the liturgical movement, create uncomfortable communities. Sometimes only the leader is not uncomfortable. The squirming that takes place during some of the community singing at Mass certainly gives the impression of discomfort. When the priest leads the group and with a mocking tone chides them for their lack of volume, particularly the men, the discomfort seems to grow — everyone but Father's, and perhaps he is relieving some of his.

Innovations always create a certain degree of insecurity. Changes in the liturgy and in the organization of the church should take into consideration man's basic tendency to resist change. More important, those who institute such changes should make allowances for the variations in individual adaptability, as well as for variations in individual participation. Being part of the community is more a psychological or attitudinal matter than it is an activity matter. Those who join in the singing are not necessarily part of the group, although they participate in the group activity. Those who refrain from various aspects of the group activity may be very much part of the group. Without even knowing it, groups establish certain rules for admission. One of the injustices that may follow is the exclusion of certain persons who have greater affinity for the group than many who follow the unwritten rules.

Finally, another kind of community is the mothering one. This is the community that may have very worthy goals, but sandwiched somewhere in the list of purposes is the proposition that members shall be taken care of as dependent children. As a misguided mother may pour all her energies into her concern for a wayward child to the neglect of everything else, so this community stands up for any member, no matter what his problem is, no matter how wrong he may be. There is no requirement for the exercise of mature responsibility; there is only the requirement of membership. There is no necessity that the individual exhibit certain character traits, only that he bear the emblem of the group. This community is as blind as the mother who believes her criminal son has done no wrong. And they defend their members as vehemently. There exists in such a group a kind of interdependency whereby the weak are protected by those a little stronger, and no one really grows up. Certain segments of American political life might be considered examples of such communities. Occasionally, a fraternal group may exhibit such attitudes. There are also religious orders that provide such an atmosphere for members.

Communities are like people, and basically like the people who compose them. There are genuine ones, and there are the phonies. There are those who bring out the best in others, those who use others, those who are used by others. Community living is a step above personal living; one must learn the latter before one can perfect the former. Community living provides the individual with the opportunity to improve himself where he is imperfect, to correct himself where he is wrong, to strengthen himself where he is weak, to give of himself to something beyond himself, viz. the image of God which he finds reflected in others — others who must remind him so much of himself.

CHAPTER V

STRESS IN THE RELIGIOUS LIFE

The life of a religious is an attempt to fit into time the truths of eternity, to encapsulate in the frailty of flesh the fact of immortality, to crystallize in humanity the wisdom of divinity. There is in every human being a spark of the divine fire; the religious life is a wish to fan that spark into a holocaust. While a spark may glow for a long time unattended and unwatched, a holocaust must burn bright or die; it must be fed or it will falter. It is to be expected that such a life should involve conflict. It is inevitable that such a vocation should entail stress.

To sacrifice one's will to that of authority, even in little things, is a situation of stress. To deny oneself the luxuries and even the ordinary comforts of an abundant society is a situation of stress. To forego the legitimate pleasures and satisfactions of marriage is a situation of stress. Are not these the factors which create stress in religious life? Is it absurd to suggest that the vows of religion are the source of overburdening stress and of ultimate religious failure? Are not the obligations that accompany the marriage vows the source of marriage failures? Every obligation carries with it the weight of responsibility. Every responsibility brings the individual to a point of conflict within himself.

The outline of stress is etched in the vows of religion. The picture is completed by the environment in which the religious lives. So here is the burden, the obligation, the responsibility, the condition of stress. Another factor must be involved in religious conflict, because stress and conflict are definitely not the same thing. It is perhaps more accurate to say that it is not the religious vows but the inability to fulfill those vows that causes unbearable conflict for the individual religious.

Others withdraw from the stress of their vocation, the burden of their responsibilities. Witness the fantastic numbers of those who cannot meet the demands of marriage vows and withdraw from them through violent quarreling, separation, or divorce. Witness those who cannot accept the basic obligations of life and withdraw temporarily through alcoholism, drug addiction or mental illness, or who withdraw permanently through suicide.

Under the pressure of deep inner conflict, under the weight of a struggle already half lost, how can the religious withdraw? To whom can she go? What release can she find? One may say, "Let her go to God to whom she has dedicated herself." She has already sought God and feels that she has not found him. She is Magdalen at the tomb, but finds not the glorious Christ. Even her spiritual dedication, that path which she thought led over the high hill of self to the valley of peace of soul and mind and heart, even that path becomes more difficult and winds ever upward beyond her strength. One may say, "Let her go back to the world if she finds this life too hard." She has separated herself from the world, and in that space and time of separation the world has truly passed her by. She who wanted to belong to Christ as everyone needs to belong to someone, she will find it difficult if not impossible to belong once more in a world she shunned. Where can she flee from the stress that overwhelms her? From the conflict that overburdens her? There is but one escape, unsatisfactory as it may be; there is but one haven to resolve a conflict too great to solve. She can become mentally ill.

Before considering some of the factors of stress in religious life, it might be well to make clear that there is an obvious method of avoiding such stress. This, of course, is to avoid the religious life. If it were possible to eliminate from religious vows those whose innate temperament or whose personality development makes them ill-equipped for the religious life, if one could eliminate these one could eliminate most religious misfits and most religious failures. How could such an elimination process be accomplished? There is no complete answer to that question. As long as the complexity of human nature plus the inscrutability of God's grace are involved the complete answer will never be found. However, since superiors do evaluate those who seek admission to their communities, it would seem proper that areas of evaluation should include the emotional stability of the candidate and her psychological aptitude for the religious life.

Many brochures on religious vocations contain a statement about the "spiritual, intellectual and physical prerequisites" for the religious life. What about the emotional prerequisites? Are the serious problems which arise in most communities due to a Sister developing tuberculosis, or schizophrenia? Do superiors lose sleep wondering what to do with the devoted Sister whose I.Q. is in the dull normal range, or does she lie awake worrying about the bright young Sister who has suddenly started to panic every time she walks into a classroom to teach? Are council meetings concerned with the lack of spiritual growth among members of the community, or are they concerned with the problem of their emotional immaturity?

Psychological testing and psychiatric evaluation of candidates for the religious life seem more and more in order. Psychological testing alone is not a suitable device for the acceptance or rejection of candidates. Neither is psychiatric evaluation an absolute criterion of emotional acceptability. A physical examination does not give absolute assurance that an applicant will not have anemia the following year or cancer in two years. The physical examination is the best method, however, of evaluating the physical health of an individual; laboratory tests are only an adjunct to that basic examination. Similarly the psychiatric examination is the best method of evaluating the emotional health of an individual; psychological tests are only an adjunct to that basic examination.

There is a question which arises in connection with the evaluation of candidates for the religious life: on what grounds can an individual actually be eliminated? On what basis can someone deny a person the privilege of entering religious life? An employer has the right to demand certain qualifications in an employee, the government has an obligation to examine carefully those who will take key positions of trust. Does God pick and choose so carefully those who shall serve him? What qualifications did he find in his apostate Peter, his adulteress Magdalen, his alcoholic Matt Talbot? Did he deny Judas the chance to serve him even though he knew that this man would not follow through on his commitment? It is doubtful whether Francis of Assisi would have passed a Rorschach ink blot test (he would have given too many animal responses), or John Vianney a Wechsler-Bellevue Intelligence test, or Louise de Marillac a psychiatric examination, or the

Little Flower a thorough physical examination. Does not the religious community exist for the glorification of God and the sanctification of souls? Is not the sanctification of its own members its first role of salvation?

The world is full of men and women who are ill-equipped physically, intellectually, or emotionally to meet the demands of life. Does the church or state forbid the diabetic to marry? Do they prevent the schizophrenic or the sociopath from assuming the obligations of the marital vows? Does not the church fight for the right even of the mental defective to bear children? How many marriages would never have taken place, how many children would never have been born, if all marriage partners and parents had to pass physical, intellectual, and psychiatric examinations? How many excellent religious and lay people might never have been born if their own good parents had been so tested to qualify for the role of parents?

There is a challenge, it would seem, to religious communities not to screen too carefully those who seek to gain heaven through their doors. These children must also seek the Kingdom of their Father. Those who are a bit weak intellectually, are a bit stunted emotionally, limp a bit physically, these must still find salvation somewhere. Why not in the religious life.?

The stress of religious life seems obvious and to point it out may be superfluous. It is important, however, for others to recognize those who have difficulty with the demands of religious life, so that the strong may help the faltering and ease their journey home. There are those entering the religious life who will find that they have considerable difficulty during their novitiate. This is a time of spiritual formation, a test of this vessel of clay. To assume that all trials during this period are of a spiritual nature is a gross over-simplification. Many of the emotional problems which will come into full bloom at a later date are budding during novitiate. The author, together with the Reverend Albert Vander Veldt, O.F.M., a good friend and a great psychiatrist, conducted some research on mental illness among religious. The first project was concerned with one hundred hospitalized clergy. The second project, which was begun just prior to the untimely death of Father Vander Veldt, was concerned with one hundred hospitalized Sisters. Of these hundred religious, a third had fairly serious, and therefore, it would seem, fairly obvious psychiatric problems during their religious novitiate. Not one of them received the benefit of psychiatric care during that period. Why is it so difficult for a Sister to get to a psychiatrist for evaluation and, if necessary, treatment? Why must she go through long periods of inner suffering and outward maladjustment before a superior in desperation or in retaliation for her behavior sends her off to a psychiatrist? Even in novitiate, why must an emotionally ill young woman be told only to pray harder and to persevere instead of being told to go to a psychiatrist? This is not being fair to the individual nor to the community involved. Psychiatric intervention *during* novitiate can prevent stress in religious life by aiding the emotional growth of candidates and by helping those who are seriously ill-equipped for the religious life to find their way out of it. Psychiatric intervention *following* novitiate can help Sisters meet the obligations of their state and relieve some of the stress they encounter.

Psychiatric treatment is not the answer for the religious who ought to pray a little harder, to stop being so willful, to accept more amicably a new assignment. Psychiatric aid might be beneficial for the religious whose deep psychological needs are not alleviated by praying a little harder, who has too much unconscious hostility to control her willfulness, who has too many inadequacy feelings to accept her new assignment graciously.

Some women are poorly equipped physically for the rigors of religious life. Teaching is regarded as a full-time job. The average teacher feels some need to relax in the evening, perhaps to go out socially, to have a weekend away now and then, and to have a summer vacation that is relaxing and refreshing. Nursing is also a full-time job. The average eight-hour shift is physically tiring. The Sister who teaches starts the day early with Mass and meditation. She may help to clean the convent before class or hurry home after class to cook dinner for her community. She may spend extra time teaching music or art or extra religion classes. During summer she frequently gives religious instructions, attends college classes in the hottest weather, and then makes a retreat just in time to return for the fall term. A Sister who is a nurse may fare equally badly. There is the same long day at the end of which she may be physically spent. Only it may not end, for her duties may carry her on into the night. The Sister who works as domestic in the convent often has hours and duties which are beyond those of the lowliest maid. There are no nights off-duty, no long evenings to watch television, not even the opportunity to slip off to her room and put her feet up, close her eyes and take five minutes rest.

It is not likely that convent life can be made radically different. The harvest is great and, indeed, the laborers are few. Those who labor must spend long hours in the vineyards. However, there are some who cannot stand the physical pace of such an active life. As a result, they may develop various chronic fatigue syndromes or even more acute physical illnesses. Too often these religious who lack the physical stamina to meet the demands of their day are unwilling to make a complaint because they fear it would be a sign of a poor religious. They suffer from their symptoms, and this suffering may, indeed, merit a rich reward in heaven. But, in addition, by not letting their superiors know of their excessive fatigue or actual physical discomfort they limit their own effectiveness, weaken their own defenses against more serious illness, prevent the relief from stress that their superiors might provide, and obviate the possibility of medical attention to remedy their ailments and correct any pathological conditions that may exist.

Just as there are those who physically cannot meet the demands of the religious life so there are those who temperamentally cannot meet them. Temperament refers to an innate psychological and physical disposition peculiar to each individual. For example, a Sister, age 52, a native of Ireland, had been teaching school about thirty years. She had always shown signs of fatigue, irritability, anxiety, low tolerance for stress. This symptomatology had, of course, caused her repeated unpleasantness with superiors and frequent ill-humored scenes with parents and children. For all of this, Sister was a devoted religious and had a sincere desire to live the fullness of her vows. In examining Sister's early life it was found that she had always been a so-called "nervous child" who needed more rest than her siblings; she became easily fatigued, and when fatigued, irritable. She was admitted to a psychiatric hospital where she was able to get additional rest and was removed from the pressure of daily duties. In these circumstances she was an amiable, pleasant, and pious woman. When she was discharged, the recommendation was made to her superior that she be allowed to take afternoon naps, sleep late in the morning, and be relieved of some of her teaching duties. It was not that Sister was a poor religious; by temperament she was just poorly equipped to be a religious.

Many young women are poorly equipped emotionally to meet the stress of religious life. One of the greatest sources of religious incompatibility is found in what is psychiatrically termed "personalty disorder." In the research study previously mentioned, it was found that about one-third of the hospitalized Sisters were there because of personality disorders. These represented only the severest cases of personality disorder, since this is not an illness that usually requires hospitalization. The majority of these personality disorders had a diagnosis of passive-aggressive personality. This diagnostic label introduces some psychiatric jargon, but this group is sufficiently common in religious communities to make elaboration regarding them worthwhile. They are characterized by either or both of two traits, dependency and hostility. Their dependency takes the form of indecisiveness, helplessness, inefficiency, clinging to the superior or to other members of the community. They behave as a dependent child toward a supporting parent. They may be a little more demanding in their dependency and exhibit stubbornness, pouting, procrastination, or passive obstructionism. In the latter case they drag their feet more obviously than the clinging child type. At the other end of the spectrum is the hostile, more openly aggressive individual who reacts to frustration with irritability, displays temper tantrums, at times is openly destructive, and has a pathological resentment of authority as embodied in superiors.

This varied description of passive-aggressive personalities must bring to mind some companion religious. It is important for one to know that this is a psychiatric entity; these unfortunate Sisters are truly ill. There is doubt as to their ability to behave differently than they do. Their personalities are truly stunted, seriously distorted. There are lacunas within the structure of their emotional life. They are torn between a desire to live as others, as mature, responsible adults, and their inability to do so. They are not children who play at being adult. They are adults who still react as children do. They suffer under the tragic awareness that something is lacking, that they are different, that they cannot quite fit into the adult world. They do not have the blissful oblivion of the psychotic nor the painful awareness of the neurotic. They have only the vague feeling of not fitting in and not knowing why.

Religious life appears as a haven for these people. Their dependency needs are satisfied by the cared for existence of community life. Their hostility is tolerated for a long time under the law of charity which surrounds them. Unfortunately even under psychiatric care their motivation is poor, their treatment is difficult, and their prognosis is dubious. It is also unfortunate that this same group would be equally poorly adjusted in marriage or in the single state. One could be philosophical about it and say that since they have to live somewhere, since they have to get to heaven somehow, why shouldn't religious share the problem of dealing with these personality disorders!

The second largest group – almost one-third – among the 100 hospitalized Sisters in the study quoted was the schizophrenic group. Characteristic of this disorder is the tendency to retreat from reality and to avoid close interpersonal relationships. The religious life seems to answer the needs of the schizophrenic or pre-schizophrenic person. It is a life to which they flee from the stress of the world and the strife of human relationships. But as every religious knows, there are many hard, cold facts about religious life. There is much give and take in the daily exchange within the community and with the world outside the community; it is neither an escape from other humans nor is it an escape from oneself.

To this group of Sisters, community living, which seemed like a haven, becomes a source of stress. They are not psychologically equipped for social interchange. They are sensitive, shy, aloof. Their coldness, their emotional detachment, their quiet manner may all seem like assets during their novitiate. Later they may become more withdrawn, suspicious, quarrelsome, fearful. The final stage is frank psychosis.

To have as a point of departure the premise that these various groups of Sisters must somehow conform to all of the requirements of the community in which they live seems to be an untenable position. Many of them cannot conform. To stigmatize them as poor religious is equally unwarranted. The notion that somehow the community must conform to them seems outlandish. One may think that such a suggestion is not only impossible, but most unnecessary.

What would happen to these same individuals in lay life? Can a marriage be dissolved simply because one of the partners has a passive-aggressive personality disorder, or a schizophrenic illness? Does society have the right to ostracize those members who cannot meet the optimum standards of life in that society? Does an institution such as a university or a hospital, does the government, does private industry have the right to disqualify for employment all who have some handicap or illness?

There will be those who cannot meet the stress of religious life either physically, temperamentally, socially or emotionally. They may break completely under that stress or they may limp along for years, ineffective and lifeless, uninspiring to others, unrewarding to themselves. To treat all religious as ideal religious is erroneous. There are many in religion who are not ideal in an objective sense. There are many who never can be. They do not have the physical strength, the temperamental stability or the emotional health to be ideal religious. Indeed, many of them cannot even be good religious from an objective viewpoint. Yet, these truly inadequate ones are perhaps better religious than those who obey all the rules, meet all the requirements, sacrifice all of self. They are striving to live a life which is beyond them; they strain to do what comes easily to others. They fail, they fall, yet they rise again to follow Christ on their *via crucis.* They push themselves up on their tip-toes to see into heaven. Perhaps the rest of mankind shall understand them better when they meet them there.

CHAPTER VI

ANXIETY IN THE RELIGIOUS LIFE

Anxiety is the mark of modern society, and the tranquilizing drug is only an inadequate response to an increasing demand for relief from this inner enemy. In decades past the accusation was often made that young men and women retreated into religious life to avoid the conflicts involved in living in "the world," and by avoiding these conflicts escape from the resultant psychological strain they cause.

Although religious life has never been free of conflict, there was a kind of dependent relationship established which gave the young religious an apparent freedom from psychological discord. The atmosphere of immutable vows, the promise of perfection through adversity, and the aegis of divine guidance through blind obedience provided a source of comfort to religious who sought relief from the anxiety of decision-making, the discomfort of uncertain tomorrows.

To seek freedom from anxiety is unrealistic, however, for anxiety is part of progress in living. The addict seeks freedom from anxiety and finds oblivion. The young adult seeks freedom from anxiety and ceases to grow psychologically or to mature emotionally. The result is a personality inadequate to meet life's demands. In the same manner, the young person who formerly entered religious life seeking freedom from anxiety found a kind of refuge from progress and a kind of darkness which was not of the soul but of the mind and of the emotions.

The number of such persons who entered religious life as late adolescents and regressed to a state of early adolescence, and settled into the security of dependent poverty, cold chastity, and dumb obedience, was relatively small; it is only that religious life provided a respectable course for such retreat and regression. The majority of religious matured emotionally and achieved a level of adulthood which was stimulated by their own anxiety to grow and was rewarded with the many anxieties of normal adult life.

At present the religious is confronted with new problems. There are fewer and fewer situations available into which the individual can retreat and avoid the antagonism of growth or the disharmony of change. Those who sought the apparent emotional neutrality of religious life found themselves face to face with controversy that intimately involved their security. Those who have matured and seek to develop more fully find variance so rapid and extensive that it is difficult to understand, much less to respond to appropriately.

Religious life has ceased to be a source of emotional security and, instead, has become a wellspring of anxiety. It is a cause of anxiety for those who are presently in religious life, for those who are considering entering, and for those who stand on the periphery. Those who stand outside formerly gazed with reverence at the religious, but now study them with a mixture of curiosity and doubt and are concerned about the confusion which vibrates through the halls of communities. These believers had, perhaps naively, thought that those halls were hallowed by the harmony of charitable living within, when it was only the sound of Gregorian chant which made it seem so.

Parents express quite well the anxiety they feel regarding a son or daughter who is about to make a momentous decision, who is caught up in the midst of a process over which he or she seems to have little control. The young son or daughter has difficulty expressing similar concern about a parent even though that concern may be just as great and just as valid. The Catholic Church, in the person of its religious, has for centuries expressed anxiety and concern over the problems and needs of the laity who are its sons and daughters. Now those children have reached a state of realistic disquietude over the turmoil that stirs throughout communities of religious men and women. Hopefully those children who represent the laymen and laywomen of the Church will have sufficient maturity not to react in haste, not to judge too quickly, not to lose filial respect.

Although anxiety seems to be regarded in our society as inimical to the happiness of individuals, it is not always so. Anxiety is the result of inner conflicts and is a signal indicating a need for change. Some situations are unhealthy and anxiety may be an indication to the individual that he should remove himself from the predicament. Some situations may be healthy and anxiety may be a stimulus for a person to readjust his attitude or his reaction to what is going on around him. Some anxieties are stirred by matters that are of serious import to the individual; others are activated by incidents or events of little or no significance. For the person who is anxious it is difficult to distinguish the true cause and especially the importance of the anxiety. To be anxious is to be uncomfortable; it is natural to seek relief from the discomfort first, and when that is achieved to be concerned minimally with why one was uncomfortable. The tooth that stops aching rarely takes one to the dentist, even though the cause of the ache is more important than the pain of it.

Religious are beseiged by many anxieties these days. There are the usual anxieties of living in a world that presents choices and their conflicts. There are anxieties peculiar to the special life of the religious. There are anxieties that are caused by healthy situations and those caused by harmful situations. There are anxieties that are deeply rooted and demand resolution; there are anxieties that are superficial and are better ignored. There are anxieties that are real for the individual because they are the product of his inner conflicts; there are anxieties that are fictitious because they are the product of associating with the anxiety of others and are not truly based within the individual.

The individual Sister may have difficulty distinguishing the importance of her anxiety and its characteristics. Is it genuine or fictitous, deeply rooted or superficial, healthy or unhealthy? There is a general rule regarding anxiety which should be kept in mind: a person tends to deal with the anxieties that have less important causes and to avoid the anxieties which are deeply rooted. Perhaps some of the areas about which religious express so much mental anguish are not the areas which are the true cause of their conscious concerns.

Young women come to the religious life with the natural motivation to become "something." That "something" is a sister, a woman who in some special way is freely dedicated to God. In addition to becoming "something," which involves the assumption of a kind of professional role, it is important that the youthful religious become "someone," which involves the development of a kind of personal distinctness or identity. This struggle to become "something" and at the same time retain or achieve the importance of being "someone" has always been a source of conflict and resulting anxiety to religious as well as to other persons who have dedicated themselves to a "cause." It is interesting and perhaps enlightening to reflect on the fact that many women religious seem to be more interested presently in what they are called than in what they are. Is there a genuine basis for concern about the name by which one is called? Or is the anxiety more truly generated by a failure to become "something" and "someone?" Is the given name by which she is called more important to her than the fact that she is called "Sister?"

In former years, religious searched within their own souls to discover God, and searched the face of God to discover themselves. The deity was the mirror into which they gazed and said, "Who am I?" Many never really found God psychologically and so never found themselves. The quest was a lofty one and promised rich returns, and it was enough that they should stumble along a road that kept them searching without answers. Today, in pursuit of being someone, they seek closer contact with their fellow man. They desire to discover the "Thou." Then, in a vain attempt to find themselves, they stare in the face of their fellow man and say not, "Who am I?" but "Who do you think I am?"

Today Sisters are involved in a study of the trappings of their lives in their search for a "something" to become. The "something" they seek appears to revolve more around the style of their habit than the meaning of wearing a habit. Some want to change their garb so radically that it is no longer distinctive of their position or their role. They are concerned that people should see them as they are and not as religious women. People used to look at Sisters because they looked like Sisters. Now they look at Sisters because of how they look to them. And that is the way people look at all other women. Should not Sisters be set apart from all other women?

It is natural to wish to be recognized as the "someone" that one is. But the religious woman has always been someone who is something, who represents something. It does her community little good, the church little good, and perhaps it is not too visionary to believe that it does the world some affront if she becomes someone who represents nothing.

Communities of religious women have some group anxiety regarding the recruitment of the young. There is ample evidence that in present-day society youth are eager for involvement, filled with idealism, conscious of commitment. How does the religious community respond to such loftiness these days? They used to respond with a call to sacrifice, an attitude of abnegation, an air of austerity. These were never equivalent to sanctity nor even contributory to a good spirit of community. Nonetheless, sacrifice, abnegation, and austerity had their own appeal and perhaps still do in this modern world. Their idealism was sometimes too starry-eyed and met head-on with the challenge of cold reality. Young people were sometimes attracted to the religious life because they had romanticized some nun teaching high school as the one truly happy, free, unsullied person they had ever known. They saw the hardships of religious life as the thorny path to that glorious goal. To be untouched by the sordidness of the world and free from the restraints of mundane needs has some appeal for youth. One can look at the hippies for confirmation. But the idealistic youth who entered it usually discovered some new realities in community life. The model nun, the prototype for sisterhood always proved to be mortal. She was not always sweet, sometimes quite unhappy, and often struggled with the limitations on her freedom.

The young sister somehow survived the blow to her idealism, because she resurrected from the ashes of her dreams the truth of her vocation and the reality of religious life. She could accept herself and her companion religious being touched by the world within themselves and within the community. The meaning of religious dedication was not altered by concerns over who sat first at table, who won favors from superiors, or who didn't do her share of work. These anxieties were not incompatible with life as a religious.

Now there are new concerns for some religious, concerns which seem to be touched by the world to the point of contamination. So many religious are deeply involved in their food and their clothing! How much money a Ph.D. or M.D. will bring to the community is perhaps considered before the spiritual benefit that might come to others. What new anxieties are created for individual religious and for communities by a shift of goals? What was the primary goal of religious life? Service? Sanctity? Was it not involved in the spiritual development of oneself and of others? What is the primary goal of religious life today, and what might it be tomorrow? Dialogue? Authenticity? Is it not becoming involved in a kind of benevolent humanism?

Religious communities have always dealt with youth, and their vocations have depended on the young. Religious communities have typically displayed a natural understanding of youth which has been a stabilizing influence in our culture. The unchanging, stable factor in religious life has been a counteractant to youthful desire for change and independence. Youth want to change their parents, their schools, the system of government, the society in which we live. Their recent behavior indicates their desire, and sometimes their demand, to change the colleges of the country. They are not yet familiar with the pain involved in the process of change. They see only the problems that require change but none of the problems in changing. In the face of this tendency of the young, reality must remain firm but not rigid. Adults must recognize that the changes the young might bring about one moment will be the victim of the next moment's whim. A situation that is unstable feeds their insecurity. There has been a stability within the church and within the religious life that set limits for man's behavior and which served as helpful guidelines to curtail the capricious wanderings of the young. The religious served as an example of stability, of the unwavering course. For this reason, as well as others, the defection of a religious was a psychologically traumatic incident to young Catholics.

The Church is in a time of transition, and the men and women of religious communities are caught up in the anxiety of change. Youth have lost much of the psychological value that religion and religious had for them. There is so little definitive response to the youth's cry of "how, where, when, why." Certainty was undoubtedly one of the attractions of the religious life. The theology of religious vocations imprinted a kind of indisputability on one's choice which could be found in no other walk of life. Religion deals with "Thou shalt" and "Thou shalt not," and the sounding board of authority is essential to the maturation of the struggling, conflicted young person.

Even after one has passed the time of adolescence and achieved a level of maturity, there remains a need for the guidelines of authority, the check-points of external rules. Understanding seems to have replaced authority as if the two were opposites to one another. Part of understanding others is to recognize that others (and oneself as well) need authoritative boundaries. The two are not opposites but counterparts. Young people are more aware of their need for understanding than they are of their need for authority. Consequently they are quick to demand an attitude of understanding and to resent its absence. Because they do not consciously appreciate their own need for guidelines and limits, they are not prone to accept authority graciously. Neither their lack of recognition of their need in this regard nor their resentment of the authoritative position should be a deterrent to the establishment of regulations or sanctions.

As rules are reviewed and changes are introduced, anxiety is stimulated especially in those who find the most security in the written regulation. During this period of study and redefinition insecurity is created. The stabilizing limits become vague; freedom suddenly seems to have new meanings, and the individual looks through the blurred boundaries to new horizons. Is this truly a period of new freedom or is it simply a time of anxious scrutiny of an area which has suddenly expanded as lines obscured?

Freedom and independence cannot be achieved in a vacuum but require an environment which provides the opportunity for growth and the occasion to alter one's choice measured against the variation in reality. Freedom must be related to reality or it is insanity. Reality has boundaries, and the propriety of behavior is bounded by the reality of external norms. In past decades it may well be true that Sisters had little freedom to express themselves. With the advent of non-directive counseling techniques, with the accent on communication, Sister may now have no end point to her self-expression. Just as she needed the opportunity to verbalize some of her feelings, she similarly needs an end point to her verbalizations. Superiors were formerly accused of not listening. Now they dare not interrupt! Freedom of expression implies the requirement that others listen. Those others, who are usually authority figures, also need some freedom of expression. And youth has difficulty meeting the reciprocal requirement of listening.

There must also be an end point to discussion in order to give some beginning point for action. Dialogue can frustrate decision, particularly when one or the other participant sees dialogue as an end in itself.

Certainly there is no new freedom for some individuals in this condition of change. For them, changes represent hardship because they cannot change within themselves. The fact of change creates an interesting antithesis: among conservatives, change brings about anxiety; among liberals, anxiety brings about change. Conservatives find change disconcerting for once change begins it is difficult to know in advance where it will end. So the very fact of change is something of a threat. When a person is threatened or made anxious he naturally reverts to the manner of behavior and method of reacting with which he is most familiar. This makes him feel more secure. As a result of this psychological tendency, when the conservative is threatened by change he turns to his conservative patterns more persistently and becomes ultraconservative. Changes which are radical and rapid are obviously more anxiety-provoking to the conservative individual because they are seen as more destructive than changes which take place gradually and subtly. It is not surprising then that some communities of religious women are creating intense anxiety among their members as a result of a so-called period of "experimentalism" which resembles more a period of anarchy.

In order to effect change it is not necessary to revert to chaos. Many changes can be decided on the basis of judgment before they are supplied in reality. One need not go through an experimental period in order to appreciate the outcome of certain kinds of behavior. Before experimenting with human beings, certain precautions must be taken and certain values must be potentially present. Any experimentation with human subjects conducted as a result of federal research grants must satisfy stringent requirements to safeguard the physical and emotional health of those subjects and to guarantee that their basic rights remain inviolate. Religious communities should take care in their "experimentation" not to jeopardize the health or the spiritual equilibrium of their subjects without justifiable cause. A study of community life from an experiential approach rather than an experimental approach should be considered.

It is evident that change causes anxiety in the conservative. That anxiety causes change in the liberal is not so obvious. One of the ways in which a person can respond to anxiety is to effect some change in his situation. Unfortunately the circumstances which are altered need not have any direct relationship to the cause of the anxiety. When one is anxious, doing something is easier than doing nothing, being active is better than being passive. It is the tendency of the liberal to believe that change is the answer to most problems. When he has a personal problem which is creating anxiety he will anticipate that some kind of change will be an effective antidote. Undoubtedly some of the changes which are being suggested and introduced in religious life today are not the result of productive thinking and prayerful deliberation, but are instead the result of the personal anxieties and inner conflicts of some of the liberal leaders. Those liberals who seek to solve their own conflicts by changing the structure of religious life or the conformation of their own community can hardly be said to have the good of the community or of the Church in mind. When they find that changes effected within the community do not relieve their own internal discord they will seek new changes, and eventually will find that they must either change within themselves or change their own vocation.

There are some outstanding recent examples of religious leaders who took the latter course of action. Some of them finally came to realize that the change must be made in themselves. They gracefully left religious life with a kind of generous acceptance of their own incompatibility to live within the limits set by that life. Others also left, but not so gracefully, not so generously, and without any recognition of their own inadequacy. They not only cling to the delusion that there can be no difficulty on their side, but they proclaim the deficiencies of their community and the religious life as such, and enter into a polemic on the Church.

The majority of liberal leaders who encourage change within their communities are sincere in their interest and circumspect in their recommendations. They truly belong to the community. They genuinely desire to improve it through change. They recognize that they need first to be part of the community and then to do something to alter its course. They have a healthy anxiety which stimulates them to work for modifications which will modernize their life but not destroy the maturity of their spiritual heritage. They are anxious to accomplish changes which will be beneficial to the community and not simply answer their personal needs. They are anxious to do things but not overanxious to get them done. They can wait for the process of change to develop gradually, rather than forcing it to occur at a predetermined rate set by their own need.

In this spirit of change youth will spontaneously and naturally be involved. The novice, junior, and newly professed respond easily to the tempo and temper of "advanced" authors. They are caught up by phrases which seem to be a direct reply to their own unspoken questions. They want to give of themselves, and people speak of commitment. They are burdened with loneliness, and people speak of dialogue. They are concerned with trusting others and a reluctance to trust themselves, and people speak of authenticity. They are still developing independence and learning how it differs from rebellion, and people speak of a new freedom. These young religious have much to contribute to the future of religious communities, but religious communities should not neglect the contribution they have to make to the future of these young religious. Leadership remains part of the endowment which maturity must give to youth. The enthusiasm and vitality of young Sisters does not equip them to determine the course of their community.

In old-fashioned communities it is still possible that the individual Sister is made anxious by her own anger and frustration. It is more likely in the newer models of community life that the anger of members causes anxiety for the superiors rather than for the angry members. The pendulum has moved from the overcontrol of hostile feelings to their overexpression. The subtleties of rebellion are thinly veneered by the charges leveled against superiors who are not considered advanced in their thinking. The religious who formerly could not deal with her inner anger because she did not realize it was there, has now come to realize it exists, but she deals with it poorly. She must still discover that disagreement does not require dissension. Authority does not eliminate authenticity or freedom, nor does anger need retribution to be relieved.

The superior who acts hastily because of the anxiety created by irritated subjects will only make herself and her subjects more uncertain of the propriety of their own feelings. Parents who are anxious about their own authority as parents are continually weakened in that authority by the whims of their children. Religious may react quickly to this comparison with the assertion that this is precisely the error their superiors make, the error of regarding them as children. Such Sisters seem to believe that there are only two conditions in life, the condition of children who are subject to their parents and the condition of non-religious adults who are subject to no one. Yet every child, especially every adolescent, knows that there are many decisions he makes which can be solely his own if he chooses to exercise his individual will, and no degree of adult tyranny can alter that condition. Every adult knows that most of life's decisions are not independent of the soft dictation of social sanction, family endorsement, and occupational ethics as well as the hard reality of employer's orders, family demands, and friends' impositions. Superiors represent only a portion of life's arbitrariness.

One of the anxieties which confronts the religious woman now more than formerly is the anxiety of adult choices. There is a spiritual simplicity in placing oneself in the hands of the superior as the interpreter of God's will. There is a psychological security in avoiding the decision-making function of adulthood by one grand commitment. So it seems. Such a commitment, however, was frequently not so much an assignment of one's will to a religious dedication as it was a resignation of one's emotional development to a level of perpetual immaturity. By this one choice, the religious was freed of making other choices. By this one expansive act of generosity, the religious gave all there was to give, and recognized no further need to generate enthusiasm, nor to develop imagination, nor to make spontaneous constructive contributions to living as a religious, nor indeed to living religiously. The only choice left was to follow.

Religious communities have for a long time — some of them from their inception — resisted this attitude among their members even though they have not successfully eliminated it. Many religious communities have attempted to preserve the self-determination of members because they have recognized the value of human beings who can think imaginatively but accept the decisions of others. They appreciate members who can live enthusiastically but have patience with the lag of life. They need religious who can contribute productively but cope with the destructive attitude of others.

Religious may have anxieties about their own volitional life, their decisions, and may also have anxieties about their non-volitional or physical existence. Psychosomatic illnesses in religious are not uncommon, and perhaps the solitude and introspective nature of convent life provides a suitable setting for such problems. In the stillness of the convent, one can hear one's heart beat and suddenly wonder, "What was that?" Most people have inner physical feelings that might be disconcerting if they attended to them carefully and concentrated on their possible pathology.

People who are interested in doing well in life usually have some anxiety about the possibility of failure. Religious have an unusually high level of dedication; it is natural for them to experience anxiety over possible lack of success. This anxiety used to involve, to an exaggerated degree, concern over the reactions of others. The present frequency of departures from religious life makes it easier to leave, in relation to the attitude of others. This does not necessarily make it easier for the particular religious to decide the issue of her own vocation. The meaning of leaving may remain a critical personal issue, unaffected by the departure of others. Does leaving represent failure? Am I choosing because of my own attitude, or am I only responding to the behavior of others? Would leaving cause greater harm to my community now because of the increased need for stable members? Is this decision a result of my own instability or a reflection of the changes taking place within the Church?

One last anxiety which a Sister may have today is the anxiety about being fulfilled as a woman. Where does Sister fit in as a woman in today's world? The Church asks this question. The world asks it. Communities are asking it. The individual Sister may ask it, and even as she states the question she gives it her own feminine style. She asks not only where she belongs in today's world but to whom does she belong. It is characteristic of a woman to want to belong to someone and be responded to. She wants to be recognized for herself. Sisters used to say they belonged to Christ, but there must be a psychological gap in such a relationship for those who are still in the purgative way. Sister may have felt this remoteness and attempted to bridge the gap by belonging to Christ's people. This gives a new kind of remoteness, for one can hardly be emotionally close to a mass of people. Perhaps Sister now needs to belong to herself so that she can keep herself not fragmented by people and activities that see her in parts, but entire and intact so that she may grow in a kind of internal expansion of charity that flows to others without losing herself or her value in that process.

The mark of femininity is the appreciation one has of oneself as a woman, the satisfaction with that fact of genetics, and the respect of oneself in that role. It is not how a woman adorns her body, but the fact that she is interested in her natural adornment which is her body. It is not how a woman relates to men, but how much she recognizes them as her counterpart. It is not how tender a woman is, but how much she values tenderness. It is not how many children a woman has or might want to have, but that she recognizes childhood as a physical and emotional state which is dependent on womanhood.

The young woman entering religion does not seek the world of competition if she regards her womanhood with reverence. The woman in religion does not know her own feminine worth if she needs to be known more as other women are known. Competition among women, whether they belong to religious communities or not, brings them an insensibility, a loneliness peculiar to spinsterhood, and the emptiness of a dedication for which there is no reward.

CHAPTER VII

PSYCHOSOMATIC ILLNESS IN THE RELIGIOUS LIFE

The life of the religious is often regarded as a struggle between the spirit and the flesh. The individual is considered to be a combination of these two forces, and by the constant war they wage with one another man's inner conflict is produced.

This point of view tries to establish the human being as an inharmonious creature destined to inevitable turmoil terminated only by death. Body and soul are set against one another as irreconcilable enemies which can work out, at best, only some fretful coexistence.

It is true there is disharmony between these two aspects of man's nature. But if this disharmony is over-emphasized, either by religious training or personality development, the result may be the cold dichotomy of a body, stripped of the glory of its own flesh and the beauty of its sensate quickening, and a soul which is housed within a barren skeleton, like a flowering cactus in the arid desert.

That there is conflict between the spirit and the flesh is obvious to the religious woman. She knows well the duality of self. When the morning bell summons her spirit to rise and adore its God, her body gently but persistently demands another five minutes of rest. At morning meditation her soul is lifted up to God in prayer, but it falters as her heavy eyelids close in a stolen moment of sleep. She understands this conflict, for it is keenly outlined in her religious life. Her spirit longs to soar heavenward, but to do this it must be free of the body which walks with leaden feet. The demands upon her time and her abilities are numerous. In the flame of charity she attempts to fulfill them all. The tedious hours of work, the weight of responsibilities engulf her. Physical fatigue overtakes the rash generosity of her soul and spends it in the idleness of repose.

There is much in the life of a Sister that reminds her of the strained relationship between body and spirit. Though the relationship is strained, it is not all disharmony for body and spirit complement one another in many ways. The body's need for rest forces the individual to limit his activity, and in that period of relaxation his spirit too is renewed. Sleep relieves physical fatigue; it also reduces mental anxieties. Exercise stimulates physical well-being, it also refreshes the mental processes. The warmth of a spring morning, the freshness of new snow, the delicacy of a flower bring prayer closer to God. Good physical health makes it easier to meet the psychological demands of life. It is easier to pray when one has a full stomach than when hungry, unless one is praying for food. It is easier to think when free of pain. It is easier to concentrate when not fatigued.

There is also evidence that the mind influences the condition of the body. A person plagued for hours by a headache may suddenly be relieved when pleasantly surprised by the unexpected visit of friends. The physical fatigue which seemed to be overwhelming to the point of immobility may fade away as the mind is caught up in the enthusiasm and fellowship of recreation.

The Sister lives in the center of the duality of flesh and spirit, of body and mind. It might be said that the religious life is an attempt to escape the bonds of the physical to capture in the frail web of time the specter of immortality. As her head nods in sleepy meditation, as her tired body kneels in distracted prayer, Sister is held in the grasp of the vise which is composed of body and soul. However, this duality is more apparent than real, for each individual is a unit. Each person functions as a unit, as a unified being. In reality body and soul are not separate entities. They cannot, therefore, be engaged in some endless struggle to overcome one another.

Soul and body are distinct principles of being according to the hylomorphic doctrine of Aristotle and St. Thomas. These dissimilar principles are united in a single being as act and potency. The soul is the substantial form and perfecting element of the finite individual. The body is the prime matter and limiting element of the finite individual. One cannot, therefore, philosophically speak of the needs of the body as distinct from the needs of the soul, or the functions of the body as distinct from the functions of the soul. Properly speaking one should speak only of the needs of the individual, whether these be for food and water, or for love and security. One should speak only of the functioning of the individual, whether this involves the force and volume of the heart beat, the violence of passion, or the production of a perfect poem.

These preliminary statements have led, by a rather devious but pertinent route, to the topic of psychosomatic life. Human beings engage in activities which are almost exclusively psychological or spiritual (using these words interchangeably only in this psychosomatic sense), activities which are almost exclusively physical, and activities which intimately involve both areas. Thought and volition are primarily spiritual functions and transcend the physical boundaries of the body as well as of external physical reality. However, in man's present hylomorphic state, thought and volition cannot be carried on without the physical substrate of the brain, which is in present reality the organ of the mind, or psyche, the structure on which these spiritual functions of the soul depend. These noblest human abilities, this intellect which can grasp the universal out of particulars and ascend to contemplate the divine, this will which can move man's body in deliberate motion and his passions in precise election, these most sublime human activities remain a function of the unified being in whom body and soul intricately complete each other.

On the other hand, the individual performs activities which are primarily physical and seem to have no participation in the spiritual element of man. One might consider the production of blood cells in the bone marrow, the growth of fingernails, or the detoxifying power of liver cells as examples of activity which is exclusively physical. Yet even these activities are not exclusively physical, because they occur through the life-giving property of the in-dwelling soul. As the substantial form of human nature, the soul is the element of existence and permeates all living cells of the body.

There is a third category of activity in which mind and body participate more actively and directly. This is the area of affective life, of emotion. By definition, emotion has two aspects. There is a definite psychological activity which consists of the perception of a situation and the feeling which results from that knowledge. There is also a definite physical response, which consists of various physiological changes within the body. The latter, the physiological reactions, are the result of the psychological changes which occur in response to a condition existing in the environment. Both the psychological response and the physical reaction must be present to fulfill the definition of emotion.

If one thinks about the flag of the United States and calmly realizes that this is a wonderful country in which to live, but if there is no physical reaction, this is not an emotion but merely a sentiment of patriotism. If one thinks about the flag and is carried away by thoughts of Paul Revere's great ride or Washington at Valley Forge, and one hears the beat of drums, the sound of bugles and cannon fire, and with all of this the heart beats faster, breathing quickens, adrenalin pours into the blood stream, one is experiencing an emotional reaction. The physiological response is present, as it must be. A person becomes "emotional" about something when he displays some of these physiological changes.

However, if there is some metabolic disturbance which causes the heart rate and respiratory rate to increase, adrenalin to flow, etc., but there is no mental disturbance, no psychic reaction, there is no true emotion.

The following analogy may further clarify the distinction. An automobile has two basic principles, both of which are necessary for it to be a functional automobile: it has a motor which is self-propelling, and it has a body structure, including wheels, which is propelled by the motor when the car is in gear. The motor is the soul of the car, the body structure is the physical counterpart. It is possible to separate the motor and the body, but when this is done the result is no longer a car. The body and soul can be separated, but when this is done the result is no longer a human being, but a disembodied spirit and a corpse. The car's motor can be started, and if the car is not in gear nothing happens to the body, except that it may vibrate a little. So it is with thought and volition. They can be set in operation without much repercussion in the human body, except for a few electrical impulses vibrating through the brain.

The motor of the car can be turned off, and, if the car is on a hill and the brake is released, the body will move along on its wheels without much effect on the motor other than to shake it a bit. Nevertheless the motor must be in the car in order to say properly that a car is rolling down the hill. So it is with the rather mechanical functions of the body. They roll along, independently of thought or will, but not without the soul being present.

Emotional life is, of course, the automobile in gear. The motor is running and the speed of its revolutions, the irregularity of its rhythm, the strength or weakness of its propulsion are all transmitted to the car body. In emotional life, the processes of thought and volition are taking place, the effective function of the mind is being transmitted to the body, and the strength and direction of the mental reactions are affecting the physical aspect of the person.

We can tax the analogy further. Emotions are in reality the strongest moving forces within man. They are the source of man's greatest power, and by nature they put him in gear. They propel him to do something, to act. When they are properly controlled and harmoniously regulated like a smoothly functioning automobile, they take the man where he wants to go. They bring him to the goals which he has set for himself in life. But, as with the automobile, things can go wrong.

Suppose an automobile is driven directly against a brick wall so that it cannot move. Or suppose a strong chain is hooked onto the body and tied to an immovable post. Or suppose the car is placed on blocks so that the wheels no longer touch the ground. Now if the motor is started and the car is put in gear, it is not going to go anywhere, but some damage may be done to it. The same thing can happen to emotions. They can occur without accomplishing any goal, but the wear and tear on the body still continues. Superiors and rules can be brick walls against which the individual cannot move forward. Morbid guilt over emotional reactions can be like a chain keeping one from progress. And when nothing can be done to relieve an emotional state, it is similar to "spinning one's wheels."

When emotions are allowed to function in their normal way they provide the individual with useful energy. This is their proper function. In their primitive form they provide preparation for fight or flight. In their refined form they prepare the person for overcoming obstacles which may stand in the way of a desired goal. In their controlled form they provide the impetus to depart from dangerous situations. For example, when a person becomes angry the digestive system slows down, the heart beats faster, breathing becomes more rapid, the adrenal glands pour their extracts into the blood stream, and these in turn act upon other body systems. The parasympathetic nervous system is dampened and the sympathetic nervous system becomes more active. All of this prepares the individual not for digesting a meal or going to sleep, nor for calmly reading a book, but for some kind of action.

The same general changes in the nervous system and endocrine products are involved in other emotions such as fear, anxiety, and sexual passion. Surely the angry person can strike a harder blow than the one who is not angry. The frightened person can run faster than the one who is not fearful. The anxious person can stay awake for longer periods than the calm person. The sexually excited person can resist physical fatigue more easily than one who is sexually relaxed.

The entire complex of human activity has been called psychosomatic in deference to the fact that man is a hylomorphic, unified organism. He is a creature whose every activity involves his psyche, or spirit, and his soma, or body. This is the *general* use of the term psychosomatic. There is a more restricted use of the term to the field of psychosomatic medicine. In this usage, the word refers to those physiological reactions which are the natural accompaniment of emotional life. Psychosomatic illness refers to those physical symptoms produced by disturbed body functioning resulting from improperly regulated emotions.

There is a true disturbance of physiology in psychosomatic illness, and there may be structural damage to bodily organs sufficient to cause long illness or to result in death. Psychosomatic illness must be distinguished, therefore, from hypochondriasis and from malingering. The hypochondriac is a person who complains constantly about imaginary physical ills. There is no physical pathology present, though the hypochondriac sincerely believes there is. It seems such a person needs to be ill. Just as some people cannot stand good news, these unhappy individuals cannot enjoy good health. It makes them sick to be well. The malingerer, on the other hand, is a person who deliberately feigns illness in order to avoid obligations or to escape from unpleasant situations. Malingerers do not *want* to be sick, they only want others to *think* they are sick. They want the benefits of illness, such as sympathy and leisure, but the pleasures and vitality of good health.

While neither of these, the hypochondriac or the malingerer, has any real physical illness – or at least not the one they are complaining about – the psychosomatic patient does have a definite change in body function and may have a change in body structure. Back pain is not imaginary. Ulcers are real. High blood pressure is a true medical concern.

In psychosomatic illness the individual may or may not be aware of the related emotional feeling that is present. A Sister may be quite aware that she is irritated by the limitations and frustrations of conventual life, and angered by the real or imagined attitude of the mother superior toward her. One Sister was in this position and found that she was bothered by stomach pains and the discomfort of indigestion every time she sat down at the community table. Here she had to face the superior. She could not escape the ordeal. The gastric symptoms were a result of the emotion of anger, which caused her digestive processes to stop functioning properly and prepared her for some aggressive action.

A great number of digestive problems are a consequence of emotional tension while eating. The child who must sit at table and be verbally abused by the criticisms of father or the condemnations of mother may make frequent trips to the doctor for unexplained nausea, postprandial vomiting, constipation or numerous other gastrointestinal symptoms. The Sister who must sit at table nursing the grudge she holds against the superior, occupied with her own brooding thoughts as the day's reading drones on, may soon be going to the doctor for the treatment of chronic stomach trouble. Dr. O. Spurgeon English says, "The mind is for settling problems and the stomach is for digesting food. But when the mind has not the personality techniques for handling formidable tasks, anxiety and insecurity increase and the stomach takes over and tries to vomit out the bad situation which cannot be mastered in any other way."

Often, however, the underlying emotion is completely unconscious to the one inflicted with psychosomatic ills. This is more likely to be the case in religious life for there is an attitude which constricts emotional expression in religious. The nun has usually come from a Catholc home where religious training was important. The authority of parents can be threatened by the rebellious spirit and belligerent attitude of children. The fourth commandment can be used as a device to control the angry reactions of children. The novitiate may increase such an attitude in the religious by indoctrinating her with the concept that disagreement means disobedience. In truth, one can obey even though one disagrees; a rule can be complied with even though it is resented.

Another factor which causes some Sisters to repress the effective part of their emotional reaction is their particular personality pattern. Individuals who have difficulty dealing with the emotional reactions involved in the intimacies of interpersonal relationships sometimes seek reprieve from the burden of such involvement by entering the convent. Their supposition that the religious life will free them from such closeness is, of course, erroneous. Religious dedication obviates the intimate relationship of marriage. Convent life permits the erection of psychological barriers between oneself and others. However, neither religious dedication nor conventual life allow the individual to escape the inevitable frictions that are part of living with other human beings. In physics, the degree of friction is influenced by the amount of contact between two surfaces. In the close physical quarters that a convent provides, and in the psychological interdependence that is part of community living, there is friction.

The religious is often poorly prepared to recognize her own emotional reactions for two principal reasons. By personality she may shy away from emotional interaction. By religious training she may have been persuaded that emotional reactions are wrong. This often applies to the emotion of anger and even more strongly to any feelings which are associated with sex. Unfortunately her acknowledgement of sex may be expanded to include any genuine emotion of love.

In emotional love – because this *is* an emotion – there are some bodily reactions taking place. This physical counterpart of affectionate feelings may be misinterpreted as manifestations of sexual interest. Confusion and guilt feelings may result. The religious must then deny the positive affection because of apprehension regarding the physical reactions. However, the physical reactions continue to occur, even after the affectionate feelings are repressed into the unconscious. A disturbed physiology may result with subsequent psychosomatic illness.

There are various ways in which emotions can express themselves physiologically. Broadly speaking there is probably no illness which is not affected by one's psychological perspective. All physicians can recall some patient whose course of illness was largely determined by the patient's will to live, or by the desire to die and be free of this world's emptiness. There are specific illnesses which are more naturally the result of chronic, repressed emotion.

Psychosomatic reactions can affect every system of the body. Skin reactions are common. If a religious cannot cope with an irritating classroom assignment directly, she may derive some satisfaction from the endless scratching which skin lesions provide. A skin disorder may prevent a young lay woman from having dates, from being popular. It thus provides her with a safeguard against some strong but repressed sexual urges.

Emotional factors often play a role in the etiology of headaches, backaches, and various rheumatic pains, or in chronic physical fatigue. In times of heightened emotion the musculoskeletal system reacts. The human is not as primitive in his posture of anger as the cat with arched back or the dog with bared teeth and stiffened limbs. Clenched fists and a generalized muscle tightening are the more human reaction. The influence of emotions on body state can be proved by clenching the fist deliberately and tightening the arm muscles as if to strike a blow. Attempting to maintain this posture for 20 or 30 minutes will cause fatigue and the muscles of the arms and hands will ache with weariness. Imagine the state of the individual who is angry all day long, and without even being aware of it is stiffening his body by tightening his muscles. Imagine the strain this puts on various joints and muscles of the body; extreme fatigue results. Smoldering resentment that cannot be recognized and must not be expressed commonly results in unexplained fatigue.

Other body systems may be involved. The respiratory system can become the target of emotional reactions. Asthmatic attacks are often precipitated by psychic turmoil. The cardiovascular system is involved in emotional life; rapid heart rate and an increase of blood pressure are common accompaniments of strong feelings. If a Sister is under constant pressure which creates anxiety for her and from which she cannot escape, she may develop chronic high blood pressure, or essential hypertension.

Repressed sexual feelings may give rise to various disorders of the female genitourinary system. Pelvic tension can result as easily from improperly managed erotic desires as back tension can result from improperly managed anger. Menstrual disorders are not infrequently the result of deep-seated emotional reactions to sexual facts. It is not unusual for a woman who is in a mental hospital to stop menstruating for the duration of her hospital stay. There are certainly psychological factors involved in the inability of some women to become pregnant. More dramatic than any of these situations is the story of pseudocyesis, or false pregnancy, in which a woman, because of some strong but usually repressed emotional needs, develops all the bodily changes which normally occur in pregnancy.

The person subject to psychosomatic illness is at an additional disadvantage in that her illness solves none of her problems. The emotional factors which are the cause of the physical ills continue unabated as long as they are not recognized and resolved in some more realistic manner. The hysterical patient whose arm becomes temporarily paralyzed because of an unconscious wish to strike someone is relieved of her anxiety by her paralysis. This type of hysterical symptom is not, incidentally, considered to be psychosomatic illness. But the patient who develops an ulcer because she drives herself unceasingly in a task she can hardly tolerate finds no relief from her burden of work, from her need to be successful, or from her resentment of her task. Her ulcer may force her hospitalization, and then for a time the burden of work is removed. The drive to accomplish and the impulse to be resentful continue unresolved.

A word of caution should be given: there is no absolute relationship between emotional illness and somatic pathology. Emotion is only one of the factors which can affect the body and bring about disorder. There are, of course, other factors which may cause high blood pressure, skin disease, menstrual irregularities, stomach conditions, etc.

The life of the religious is replete with the possibility of psychosomatic illness. There are two principal causes for this plethora. First, the religious is trained, at least by implication, not to express emotion directly. Laughing is frowned upon as worldly in some novitiates. Weeping may be considered incongruous with a spirit of detachment. Anger may be regarded as disrespectful and disobedient. Physical affection may be judged universally sexual and so invariably sinful. (Then what of the physical affection a mother feels for her child?) Resentment of an assignment may be frowned upon as rebellion against God. Feelings of frustration may be interpreted as lack of generosity. (It may be exactly because of a great generosity that one feels so frustrated!) In this environment which denigrates emotional expression, the religious is forced to restrict her emotional life and to repress many of her emotional feelings. Feelings can be restricted but not renounced. They can be repressed but not removed. An angry person can be subdued by an authoritarian superior, but her anger cannot be silenced, for it will speak through the red fire of a skin rash or the burning flame of a stomach ulcer. Sorrow can be denied by an individual, but, if refused the lacrimal gland, it may do its weeping through some inner gland, and diabetes or hyperthyroidism may result.

The second principal cause of psychosomatic illness in religious is its respectability. There is only one thing worse than displaying emotions and that is to display emotional instability. Going to a psychiatrist is probably feared almost as much as going to hell. It lacks only the eternal commitment. Going to a psychiatrist makes the present situation a sort of living hell. Superiors are suspicious forever after. Other religious are superficially sympathetic but they always watch out of the corner of their eye, as if they secretly hope for a few scenes from psychosis to be enacted at any moment. There is always the inner struggle for the religious who sees a psychiatrist. "Does this mean I'm a poor religious? How have I failed?"

By contrast, how wonderfully wonderful it is to be physically ill. The doctor prescribes medicine, perhaps a diet if one is lucky. Everyone knows that Sister is sick. She looks sick. (It is the special cross of neurotics that they always look so well.) She may be physically ill in the hospital, or she may have to stay in bed in the convent because she is physically ill. She gains a reputation for being physically ill. She can console herself that it is so much better than being neurotic, as she lies there unknowingly nursing a psychosomatic illness. Medication seldom cures psychosomatic illnesses; it only relieves one set of symptoms. Another set will soon appear. The patient goes through a litany of symptoms with the prayerful response to each being "Blessed are those who are physically sick."

Psychosomatic illness can best be treated by dealing with the emotional problems which cause it. The doctor must be wise enough to perceive these emotional problems, and the community must be kind enough to accept them. The patient must be energetic enough to grapple with them.

Psychosomatic illness can best be prevented by allowing, yes, even encouraging religious to express their emotions in a healthy manner, to cope with them in a socially suitable fashion, and to sanctify them in a spiritually acceptable way.

CHAPTER VIII

ANGER IN THE RELIGIOUS LIFE

There are many special problems which occur in the religious life, and there are some special community rules or attitudes to help the religious solve her special problems. There are many special temptations in the religious life, and there are those special graces of the state which help the religious resist those temptations. There are many special crosses in the religious life, and there are those special compensations which make the yoke of the religious less burdensome.

There is an area which seems to involve all three of these, for it can be regarded as a problem, as a temptation, and as a cross. However, it is difficult to circumscribe this problem; it is an intricate task to delineate its morality; it has a mysterious way of being a cross. Sometimes one isn't even aware that one carries it, and all the while it exacts a toll in troubled hearts and community turmoil. This special, difficult subject is anger, or hostility. The general topic of anger is well worth recognizing within the religious community, for this tree of fury spreads many branches into the lives of individual religious and the spirit of religious houses.

There are various objects of anger in the religious, and they shall be considered one by one. Anger may focus on one's superiors, on one's peers, on God, and on oneself. There are peculiar psychological implications in each of these reactions.

By way of clarification it should be mentioned that anger is not being examined from a *theological* point of view but from a *psychological* point of view. We are not concerned here with the sin of anger, but with the sensation of anger. We are not appraising anger as just or unjust. How does anyone in the frailty of his own humanity have the right to be angry at another who is only more frail than he! When a person tries to justify his anger, it seems more likely that he is trying to excuse it. An attempt to justify anger brings it into an intellectual frame of reference. There it loses the flavor and force of its emotional tone. Must anger be just to be respectable? Anger need have no reason for being, it simply is. It need have no justification for occurring, it simply happens. As it is, as it happens, it must be resolved.

Anger is human nature's primitive response to hurt, whether it be physical or psychological. It is principally a stimulus-response phenomenon. If someone is deliberately pushed downstairs, he becomes angry. If someone is tripped by accident and falls downstairs, he is angry also. Justice has little to do with it. If the superior sends a Sister who has been teaching high school chemistry for ten years to teach reading in first grade, Sister is angry. The vow of obedience does little to alleviate that basic response of resentment.

This feeling of anger, this rising resentment appears to be morally indifferent. It is like the feeling of hunger when one's stomach is empty. The feeling is there. There is no harm in admitting it. What one does about that hunger can be morally good or morally bad. One can eat meat and break the law of abstinence; one can commit the sin of gluttony; or one can take some legitimate nourishment in legitimate quantity and thus relieve the feeling of hunger. Anger is like the pain a person gets when she stubs her toe, bumps her hip on the corner of a desk, or pricks her finger on a thorn. The pain is there. One can scream about it, swear about it, cry about it, dance around on one foot, or rub the sore spot. For some reason, any of these activities seems to help, and the pain decreases.

This primary feeling of anger is there when a Sister stubs her toe of willfulness against the rock of authority, or when she bumps her pride on the corner of cold reality, or when she finds that some rosy assignment is really full of thorns. The anger is there. She can scream about it, swear about it, cry about it (and many women cry because of anger), dance around on one foot about it; but she can't rub it. However, she has a good substitute for rubbing. She can get it to blossom out in a flaming skin rash and then scratch it night and day, or she can get it to burn a hole in her stomach and try to extinguish the fire with internal ablutions of various antacids.

Sister's anger can have various objects. In fairness to all concerned, first consideration should be given to superiors who, at least in this hierarchy, have primary place. Superiors represent authority. As such they personify the strict father, the cruel mother, the mean grandmother, the crabby school teacher of childhood. The attitude of the average religious toward superiors is undoubtedly influenced by her earlier attitudes toward authority figures. Many of the severe problems among religious in conflict with superiors are directly traceable to problems they had as children with their parents.

Since superiors represent authority figures, it is natural that this relationship should prevail. However, there are additional factors which foster this authority-subject relationship and which make it a dangerous dilemma for the average religious. Superiors represent authority and as such, their subjects must make many requests of them. The religious of the community have most of their basic needs satisfied through the authority represented by the superior. Such a single source of satisfaction for one's needs is almost limited to religious life. It is obvious that this situation puts the religious in a position of dependency.

It is a characteristic of mature adults to treasure their personal independence. But while in fact everyone is dependent on others in many ways, it is not often that someone is dependent on a single individual for the fulfillment of many different needs. Most people are in a sense dependent on others to sell them clothes, groceries, to build their houses, and so on. Rarely is a person dependent on one individual to do all these things. If one doesn't like his clothier, he can go to another. If one doesn't like his house, he can buy another. The religious does not have the freedom of choosing the person on whom she might be dependent, nor are the objects of her dependency so multiple. She is forced into a dependent role without choice of counterpart.

There are few things in psychiatry or in medicine – even in the world – that are universally true. One formula in psychiatry comes close to that universality. It is this: wherever one finds dependency, one finds hostility on the other side of the coin. Therefore, the stage is already set by the very structure of community life. Hostility is almost a natural result in a setting of such dependency. Although the vow of obedience requires her to do so, imagine the natural chagrin of the Sister who goes to her superior to ask if she may buy a 75¢ paperback book for a class she is taking, and the superior says, "No, it isn't necessary." Here is a thirty-five year old adult female with high intelligence and a master's degree in science being refused a request for a 75¢ supplemental book! This is an example of the dependent role in which religious are placed by their vows. There is no question of whether it should be so; this is one of the sacrifices of self that religious life entails. Sisters may forget the supernatural motivation for this relationship and resent the sacrifice. Even if they can accept it, or at least tolerate it intellectually and spiritually, they are almost certain to resent it emotionally and feel angry about it.

The healthy relief of that anger depends on the individual religious and on the superior. There are some parents who can get very angry themselves but tolerate no show of anger on the part of their children. And there are some superiors who stand so rigidly on the letter of obedience that their subjects' anger is controlled only by a second emotion which can be equally disturbing – fear.

A superior can do so much to alleviate the inner pressure of anger by suggesting to Sister that she must accept her [illegible]ssion but must not necessarily like it. In fact, it might be a good idea to encourage Sister to express her real feelings about an assignment or some administrative decision. If this is to be successful, Sister must have the ability to express her anger in an acceptable manner, and the superior must have the ability to accept it graciously.

It is true that some people in authority cannot tolerate the anger of their subjects because they are insecure, either in their position or in their decisions. The superior who refused the 75¢ book might well object to Sister getting angry, because she knows the basic weakness of her own position. If everyone in the community smiles sweetly and agrees softly when the superior makes a pronouncement, the superior is less inclined to doubt her own perfect wisdom than if someone frankly disagrees or displays indignation. When authority is insecure, it becomes more absolute, and when it is unwise, it becomes more unbending. The superior who rules with an iron hand and allows no back-talk gets the same results as do strict parents – the silent rage of laziness, the open rebellion of misbehavior, the resentful retreat of running away – and running away for the religious can mean leaving the community.

Some people cannot tolerate their own anger. Just as superiors must be encouraged to accept the anger of their subjects, so must they encourage subjects to accept their own anger and to express it in healthy ways. The following is an example of an angry Sister who had been eight years in the convent. She had been an extremely dependent person, constantly making demands on her successive superiors. She would stay in bed mornings, feigning illness, so that the superior would come to see her. The superior often brought her a tray and sat for long periods keeping her company. If the superior did not come, but sent someone else, the Sister would cry most of the day and stay in bed longer. She was, of course, angry, but couldn't recognize it or express it. As her demands for attention from the superior increased and became less subtle, she would practically order the superior to come to her room to see her. Finally, she threatened to drink lye if the superior did not spend more time with her. The situation had now become intolerable to the superior, and psychiatric help was requested. During psychiatric care, Sister came to see more clearly the fact and force of her anger. She had not controlled it formerly, but merely channeled it subterraneously where it eroded the soil of her good intentions and disintegrated the rock of her dedication. As she became more aware of her maneuver, it became less successful. Finally one day her anger came to the surface and shot out like a geyser. In the presence of several other Sisters in the community she called her superior a "big, fat slob." Perhaps the superior deserved the remark not because she was a big, fat slob (although she was a bit plump), but because she had been afraid of this Sister's anger and had subjected herself to Sister's demands without ever having helped her face her anger more directly at an earlier date. Sister had been considering leaving the religious life and by this time her decision to do so was fairly definite. It was a good thing it was, because within a few hours after her outburst she was removed from that house, and within three days she was put out of the community. This reaction on the part of her superiors displayed their immature intolerance of anger. Although far from the best, that is certainly one way of controlling the angry outbursts of one's subjects.

Parents frequently impress on their children that they must not get angry. The children learn that getting angry causes their parents to disapprove of them severely, sometimes completely. Such basic disapproval is difficult for a child to tolerate, so he cannot tolerate his own anger. He feels guilty about it, ashamed of it, and flees from it. Even while his parents are forbidding him to get angry, they are bursting out with anger at each other, at the neighbors, at all the "fool drivers on the road," etc. This attitude indicates to the child that anger is acceptable when coupled with authority. Children reared in such a situation have sufficient trouble with anger. Their problem is increased in the Catholic home where "Honor thy father and thy mother" is often interpreted, especially by parents, to mean "Don't become angry at father and mother." After this indoctrination, the final seal of disapproval is placed on anger when in novitiate the young nun is taught by implication that "obedience" means "not getting angry".

Children have no right to get angry. Neither do Sister subjects. But why does one need a right to get angry, when none is required to feel pain, to get hungry, to be cold. Rather than teaching children not to get angry, parents ought to be teaching them, by words and by example, how to get angry and get over it. Superiors might do the same with their subjects.

Sisters who cannot express their anger may be fettered by long-forgotten fears of parental disapproval or shackled by phantasies of serious sin. The scriptural admonition "Let not the sun go down upon your anger" is sound advice psychologically. It is much better to have it out and have it finished. Anger which smolders, lives and thrives.

For the physical protection of superiors and the continuity of insurance policies against destruction of the convent, one should hasten to add that anger must be directed into healthy forms of release. A direct but controlled expression of anger in words is certainly a healthy outlet. Physical activity which provides a lessening of physical tensions associated with emotion is of benefit to many. Roller skating in the basement, a brisk walk, some folk dancing, a dart board, indoor horseshoes, all can be supplied on a modest budget. It is regrettable that every convent is not equipped with a swimming pool and a complete gymnasium.

Sisters not only have hostile feelings toward superiors but they are also caught up in the daily friction of rubbing elbows with one another, in the petty jealousies that permeate their day-to-day living, in the conventual conflicts that are small replicas of political prototypes.

The relationship of a Sister to her siblings in her childhood is often reenacted in her community life as she relates to the other Sisters in the convent. If Sister had a brother or sister of whom she was jealous, it is an easy step to become jealous of other Sisters. If she resented a sibling because favoritism was shown toward that sibling, she may be quickly resentful of the superior's attention to another religious. If she was the favorite at home, she may be angered if she cannot continue in that privileged position.

In their interpersonal relationships with others, Sisters sometimes express their hostility toward the superior. When children are strictly controlled by rigid parents and not permitted to voice their anger, the home is often filled with an unusual amount of fighting and quarreling among the children. They are quite obviously getting their anger out at one another even though they may not be the source of one another's anger. It is not difficult to imagine that when a Sister, unable to vent her anger, is sent on a mission which she bitterly resents, she may make everyone in the house miserable by her irritability and vile moods, her generally disgruntled demeanor. If she could once express her bitter resentment over a new assignment, she might feel a great deal better about it. Complaining secretly to another Sister may not bring much relief, because she then has the guilty feeling that she is being uncharitable to mother superior. Even more important, she does not have the satisfaction of letting mother superior know that she is angry.

There is a particular type of dependency which may appear among Sisters as well as among lay people, and it breeds a subtle kind of anger. This is psychological dependence. It exists when one's attitude about one's self is dependent on the attitude of others toward one's self, when one's mood and opinion is dependent on the mood and opinion of others. Psychological dependence makes one truly subject to the influence, to the will of another. The dependent Sister is pleased with herself if one of her friends is pleased with her. By this same dependence, she goes out of her way to please a particular friend so that she may bask in her affection. The dependent Sister is happy when her friend is happy or sad when her friend is sad, as her moods are fastened to the moods of another.

As usual, this coin of dependency has its other side — hostility. It is not pleasant to feel that one is the pawn of another, the victim of another's whims. This is the lot of the dependent Sister. She rebels against that situation through resentment that must be concealed, through bitterness that must remain coated with sweetness, for the need to please does not permit her to show anger.

Everyone is dependent on God. The religious takes on, by way of sacrifice, additional dependencies on superiors and the community. But *psychological* dependency of the kind mentioned is always unhealthy, usually a handicap to spiritual progress, and frequently a disrupting influence on community spirit.

Encouraging Sisters to think independently, training them to accept responsibility singly, teaching them the emotional hazards of Sisterhood might help them resist the quiet infiltration of dependency needs before these needs stifle individual growth and dampen the spontaneous, natural spirit of sodality.

In addition to anger toward superiors and other Sisters of the community, religious are sometimes unconsciously angry at God. Fortunately, this does not occur frequently. Occasionally a person in religion feels that she *had* to become a religious, that God practically ordered her into this blessed servitude, that she had little free choice in the matter. If this Sister is more impressed with the servitude part of the life than she is with the blessed part, she is faced with a definite conclusion: she has been forced into an unpleasant life of subjection and deprived of the opportunity to enjoy many of the things in the world outside. Such an attitude can only result in feelings of anger toward God. In the life that she has chosen, or rather that she feels has been thrust upon her, such feelings are completely incompatible. They must be hidden even from herself, especially from herself. So they become unconscious.

Unconscious feelings continue to influence behavior. Sister finds religious exercises not only tedious but actually unnerving. She may say to another, or more likely think to herself, "If it weren't for all the praying and spiritual exercises, I would be very content in this life." She is like the Sister who cannot deal with her hostility toward superiors and says, "If I didn't have to go to mother superior to ask for things all the time, I'd be happy as a religious." In the same manner, the Sister who feels unconsciously hostile toward God for having trapped her in religion is saying, in her statement about prayer, that if she didn't have to be going to God to ask for things all the time, she would feel a great deal more comfortable.

It is important to understand that periodic distaste for spiritual exercises is not an indication of this kind of hostility toward God. In addition, this type of anger or resentment is not nearly as frequent among religious as are the other two types – anger toward superiors or peer religious.

From a psychological point of view, scrupulosity is a problem which shows rather vividly the transfer of feelings from parental figures to God, and the manner in which hostility can be subtly expressed. The scrupulous person has considerable hostility. What should one person think if another regards him as an extremely severe taskmaster with a heart of ice? What should one person think if another accuses him of total lack of understanding, an absence of sympathy, an unwillingness to be satisfied no matter how much is done? One could certainly consider that other person hostile. This is exactly the attitude of the scrupulous person toward God. Of course, it is an attitude which they have displaced from parental authority to divine authority.

The final object of anger to be considered is anger toward one's self. There are several ways in which this can be manifest, two of which are particularly important. The first is self-disparagement, the second is depression. Self-disparagement is sometimes used as a device to obtain praise from others and as such can be considered an indirect grandiosity. But the one who deprecates herself may be truly feeling a serious absence of personal worth, or she may be trying to bolster a faltering sense of worth by forcing compliments from others. As a child she may have been deprived of that solidarity of spirit which would have come from knowledge that she was loved and respected for what she was, and not being weighed constantly in the balance for what she could produce.

Children who have been rejected by their parents — one or both — may come to reject themselves. Many of the attitudes held by adults were learned as children from their parents. This is evident in peoples' patriotism, in their prejudice, in their attitude toward work and toward religion, and it is also found in their attitude toward themselves. Their basic rejection of themselves, their anger at being who they are, their distaste for being at all — these may all be safely concealed from the world and even from themselves. They are indirectly indicated through various self-destructive devices. These people may destroy themselves psychologically by their self-depreciation. They may even look for reproof from others and delight in disapprobation. This may be mistaken for humility or meekness. It is neither! It is sickness! They do not practice self-denial or submission, for in their own minds they have nothing to relinquish, and servitude is only what they deserve. They get others to reject them so that their anger toward themselves can be partially appeased.

It is characteristic of self-destructive people that they cannot survive success or accept appreciation; they cannot permit themselves to be happy. An example is the Sister who was convinced that she was ultimately doomed to hell and that she deserved it. Each time she reached a point where she was making a good adjustment, something would inevitably occur to place her once more in a precarious position within her community. It is not uncommon to find this self-defeating mechanism in operation among religious.

There are other ways in which anger toward self is exhibited. Some people are accident prone. They not only fall down, they manage to get hurt. They never have the opportunity to witness an accident, they always happen to be in on it. Others find their need to attack themselves satisfied through physical illness. They do not get colds, they contract pneumonia. They do not get headaches, they suffer migraine. They do not have indigestion, they develop ulcers.

A young nurse who was in psychiatric care was filled with hostility toward herself. She drove herself mercilessly and then complained of all her physical ailments. She ate a markedly inadequate diet and allowed herself as little sleep as possible, usually two or three hours a night. When she was on duty she was an excellent nurse. She didn't walk, she ran. She didn't ask anyone else to do what she could find time to do herself. She tried to do it all and stayed as long as two hours after the change of shift, finishing her work. When she was off duty, she scrubbed and painted her apartment, made clothes, washed everything by hand, and so on and on. When she had one apartment completely clean, she would move and start on another. One might think that this girl simply had a compulsion to work. Her compulsion really was to destroy herself and she had nearly succeeded in doing so a few years before by an overdose of sleeping pills.

There are Sisters who refuse to relax, who ignore the basic rules of physical and emotional health, who drive themselves in a manner that is fatiguing, and sometimes frightening, to those who watch because others often sense the self-destructive quality of such industry.

The ultimate depth of anger at one's self is found in depression. This is typically an illness of middle age, but it is also found in late adolescence to a surprising degree. The most common cause of depression is anger toward others that is completely frustrated in its expression and is consequently turned against one's self. This anger toward self is therefore different than the anger discussed above, because the primary object of this anger is others; it is only secondarily directed toward one's self.

Teenagers who become filled with rage against adults and who do not find some outlet for that rage in controlled expressions, angry outbursts, or delinquent behavior, may turn this anger on themselves and take their own lives in direct suicide or in the indirect suicide of wild auto rides, dangerous drugs, and dare-devil behavior that jeopardizes their lives and frequently ends in death.

Similarly, adults who are unable to project their anger onto its proper object may focus it inwardly. The result is depression. The final outcome may be suicide. It is likely that young adults, with their greater resilience, initiative, and spontaneity, ward off more effectively the inversion of anger. Life holds more interest for them, it carries them forward almost against their will. But as middle age approaches, the human being begins to run down a little. The main spring is becoming less taut. One can no longer drain off anger easily through the vent of activity. Life holds less adventure, and the future holds less promise.

Against this changing scene a Sister may look once more at her anger and find that, as with so many other problems in life, there is no use resisting any more. Energy runs low and the inner push that it takes to get outwardly angry is somehow lacking. It does not seem worth it. When middle age comes along, a person begins to avoid exertion; one drinks the warm water at hand, rather than walk a flight of stairs to the cold fountain. One decides not to read a book just now, rather than to go to the library to get it. Anger is managed in somewhat the same manner. It is so much easier to attack one's self than to attack another person who is the object of the anger. Besides, there is little danger of a struggle this way, because one really does not feel like fighting back against oneself.

These are the natural occurrences which bring about depression. There are additional factors operating in the religious life. People in their late thirties, forties, and early fifties, are less flexible than they used to be. They do not adapt as quickly; they do not adjust to change quite as easily. In the religious life, this age group has passed the period of development and is now thought to be well established in the vocation. This age group is given the more difficult missions. The younger nuns are protected, and if they do have a difficult mission their enthusiasm and vitality carry them through it. The Sisters in their late fifties, sixties and older are protected partially by age or perhaps by some rank they may have achieved. If they are given a difficult mission, they may look at it a bit more philosophically from the advantage of their years; or they may refuse it with the obstinacy and the impunity of seniority; or they may accept it graciously but escape it through some legitimate illness.

This is the outline of anger as it may affect the lives of the religious. Little has been presented about the control of anger. More important than control is proper expression. Anger can be regulated in an adult manner. In order to be regulated it must first be recognized. Sisters sometimes have crying spells, or sleepless nights. They may feel like running or that they're going to explode. Any one of these or many other symptoms may be an indication of an underlying hostility. There are only two great reservoirs of emotional impulse that create conflict for human beings: the sexual impulse and the aggressive impulse. The latter causes much more havoc in the religious life than does the former but little attention is paid to it.

Once anger is recognized, it should be released in a proper way and on its proper object. Arguing with someone, expressing an opinion even heatedly, slamming a book down, banging a door, telling someone directly that you are angry – these reactions seem hardly sinful. If anger can be recognized and released then it need not be displaced from mother superior to companion Sisters, or from humans to God.

Finally, if one can learn to accept with tranquility one's own limitations, there will be less reason to get angry at oneself. If one can maintain the equilibrium, that a sense of humor provides, there will be less reason to get angry at mother superior. If one can maintain the equanimity that true humility brings, there will be less reason to get angry at one's companions in religion. If a Sister can acquire the simplicity that faith alone can give, she will know that she cannot be angry with God.

If you accept yourself, if you have a sense of humor, if you possess humility and simplicity, your anger can never be great and can never do real harm. Even though it fills you, it will leave you. And when it is gone, you will find within your heart the love which only seemed to be absent.

CHAPTER IX

LOVE IN THE RELIGIOUS LIFE

Love has as many definitions as there are lovers in the world, perhaps more, because there are those who love with difficulty but use the word with ease. Because of its complexity it is important to distinguish what might be called levels of love. There is the intellectual virtue of love which is an attitude of benevolence and beneficience toward another. There is the psychological condition of love which involves an appreciation of and an attraction toward another. There is the emotional state of love which is more a feeling of attraction than an evaluation of attractiveness. There is the purely physical aspect of love which is a response to an object of sensual appetite.

One can love at any one of these levels separately or one can combine two or more of them in a relationship called love. Obviously some love relationships are simply sensual. Others are purely platonic. The religious who seeks a union of love must be aware of the level on which that union is formed and not confuse the realities of the relationship through use of the ambiguous term love.

Although one can consider kinds of love, characteristics of love, and objects of love, there must be some common understanding of the word which people accept in its everyday use. Is there a generally accepted idea of what love is? Or does the use of the term only cause confusion by suggesting a customary meaning which in fact does not exist? Doesn't each person give his own meaning to the word even when it is used by others? When a mother speaks of her love for her child she probably means something quite different from that which the child understands by her statement that she loves him. The mother may be thinking of the burden which love brings, but the child may think only of the comfort it provides. Any two people who profess to love one another may be approaching each other at different levels, not finding a union in love but only a conflict in interests. The expectations which each one has of the other are largely determined by each one's own concept of love.

The religious who sets out to find a bond of love at the intellectual level may find herself bound to someone whose level of loving is a sensual one or at best an emotional one. It is easier for the person seeking an intellectual plane of love to descend to the valley of sensory attachment than it is for the person who seeks sexual satisfaction to rise to an awareness of a more profound union. The person who knows the completeness of an ideal love has a natural appreciation of the components of human relationships. The person who has become absorbed only in the sensory manifestation of love may be relatively insensitive to the consummation of love at other levels.

Whatever difficulties exist in accurately defining love, its presence in our lives both as a term and as a psychological fact is obvious. A book on human ecology published recently has as its thesis the idea that there is a single principle governing the entire gamut of human behavior; that one principle is called the principle of least effort. The author states, in effect, that human beings invariably take the course of action which will involve the least expenditure of energy in the final analysis. He goes to great lengths to verify this conclusion by many supporting examples. It is singularly interesting that the word "love" is found neither in the index nor in the text itself.

When one speaks of human behavior, it is difficult to proceed very far without using the word love, or searching for an equivalent term. If it were not for some level of love which motivates each of us, we might well function according to a principle of least effort. Love moves individuals to expend effort beyond need and to strive for that perfection of love which requires the maximum endeavor. Yet love is effortless. There is no exertion in loving, although loving may bring one to great strain and great labor. Love lifts a person to the kind of dedication and the degree of activity which achieve life's highest goals. Yet love attains its greatest goal in the act of loving rather than in the accomplishments of loving. Contemplative communities have served as examples of love in its noblest as well as its severest form.

A human being is a complicated system of drives, needs, and abilities; he cannot be summed up under one principle. He has two great faculties which make him especially human: the ability to think, and the ability to love. It is not his power to think, but his potential to think which is his pride as a human. It is not the manner in which he loves, but his capacity for loving which establishes his human dignity. The child who does not study and does not learn is, therefore, as important as the child who reasons well and learns much. The retarded child or adult has an impairment in his power to think, but the fact that his soul will someday be able to know God indicates its potential for knowledge. It needs only to be free from the shackles of a body which by imperfection is a handicap, of a brain which by infirmity is a barrier.

Just as a person may have a limited intelligence quotient or "think power" it is also possible to have a limited emotional quotient or "love power." The brain is the organ of the mind and must necessarily be intact if a person is to think correctly and completely. It may be deficient due to hereditary factors, impaired as the result of injury, or enfeebled because of illness. If it is damaged to any serious degree, the thinking power of the mind will be diminished. The brain is also involved in the complex act of loving. It seems logical to suppose, therefore, that a person's power to love can also be impaired by some organic deficiency in the brain.

There is substantial evidence in psychological research that the intellectual functioning of a person may be greatly altered by environmental experiences. The same may be true for one's ability to love. Early deprivation of basic requirements may seriously restrict a person's capability for expressing love and for loving another. The mother's love for the child is first communicated in a tactile manner. Intrauterine life must have its tangible satisfactions. The caring activities of the mother for her newborn stimulate the sense of touch principally. Suppose that a particular newborn had some abnormality in which the sense of touch was impaired and more painful than soothing. This would surely result in an obvious problem in such a baby's later ability to love and be loved.

We are far from being pure rational beings. Many of our reactions involve unspoken emotional exchanges with other persons. It is quite possible that we respond to others more quickly and more sensitively in their capacity to love than in their capacity to think. The power of thinking is of particular value to the individual himself; the power of loving is of particular value to others. The ability to feel something which cannot be put into words and to know that one feels it, the fact that one tear can be more expressive than a thousand words, the inner knowledge that one is somehow ultimately caged within oneself until someone else finds the gate which no words could ever open – such realities may seem unreal but love knows they exist. The person who has this experience of loving will anticipate a similar reaction in others. Strangely, the individual is not disturbed by the fact that others do not think at his level. He does not expect that they necessarily will. He is expectant that others will love as he does. He will even deceive himself to believe that they do. The expectations of one who loves may be beyond the limitations of the one who is loved. The "love quotient" of one may be at a much different level than the other.

Just as there are those who are without the power to think, there may be those who are without the power to love. The two need not be correlated. The mentally retarded may be deeply affectionate and loving. The highly intelligent may be without genuine attachment. In fact, the use of reason may often disguise the absence of love. Words are more at the command of the faculty for thinking than of the faculty for loving. One can speak of love because reason dictates an advantage in doing so, but words of love cannot create a reaction that does not exist. Love can be communicated easily in silence. Ideas are communicated through words and it is important to exchange ideas with one's friends and especially with one's enemies. Words can break down the barriers to love, but they cannot provide the bridge that carries the force of love.

Religious are involved in the new cult of communication in their quest for love. The Sisters' concern about their need to love is something like the comedian's concern about his need to laugh. Laughing is his business. Though he may not laugh in quite the same way others laugh, though he may be more aware of their laughter than he dare be aware of his own, though he may laugh the most when he feels it the least, he does it well. The more he concentrates on his own need to laugh, the more difficult it is for him to do so and the more artificial it becomes. As a result, the less his need seems satisfied. For the religious, loving is her business. Though she may not love in quite the same way others love, though she may be more aware of their loving than she dare be of her own, though she may love the most when she feels it the least, she does it well. The more she concentrates on her own need to love, the more difficult it is for her to do so and the more artificial it becomes. For her, too, the less her need seems satisfied. Many Sisters concentrate too much on their need to love.

Because of their concern about loving, religious are captured by the intellectual approach to loving which commits one to love the poor, the people of God, the members of minority groups, the whole world. One can love the idea of loving such large groups, but the commitment is beyond the depth of meaningful love. The intellectual virtue of charity can and should encompass all men, but just as the comedian is grandiose to wish the whole world for his audience, so the religious reaches beyond her limits in trying to love the whole world. Even the Flying Nun cannot accomplish such feats.

Words of love are sometimes only love of words; the broad commitment may cloak a tangle of betrayal. Peter spoke so eloquently when he said, "Lord, to whom shall we go? You have the words of eternal life." He spoke so evasively the language of human love when he said, "I do not know the man." Isn't it possible that he loved Christ more in his betrayal of him than in his earlier commitment to him? Isn't it also likely that Christ loved him more at the time of the betrayal? Some religious who have not found love within the structure of their communities have searched the broad expanse of popular concepts and encompassing commitments. Some have been quickly disillusioned, not with the ideas but with the lack of meaningful love. Some leave the religious life to seek a love they could not find within it. It is possible they love God more for doing so. Others have not found love within the religious structure of old or within the framework of some liberal renewal; nor will they find it in leaving the community, because their capacity to love and to respond to love has been genetically damaged or environmentally diminished. The fact that one may not have found love in the religious life does not indicate a lack of love within that environment. There are many who never find love because of their own inability to recognize it or respond to it.

A rather basic characteristic of human nature is a resistance to loss of control. People have an innate fear of losing control over themselves. Fear of mental disease occurs in most people and is related to this concern over losing control. Fear of death, fear of anesthesia are other examples. Sleep represents a loss of control, and those who are acutely anxious about losing control may become afraid to go to sleep. Anger may represent loss of control and be avoided for that reason. Avoidance of laughter may become part of an overcontrol. Human beings desire to maintain self-control, to be self-possessed. Thinking and loving present an interesting paradox. By reasoning, one maintains control of oneself. By loving, one relinquishes some control to another. Since the individual naturally resists loss of control, there is a tendency to resist love because it makes the individual at least partially subject to the loved one.

To love, therefore, is to give up part of oneself, to give oneself to someone else. A Sister's conflict over obedience would be so easily resolved if she loved her superiors, her community. This love provided the resolution for many Sisters who saw God in their superiors. Loving God made obedience gentle because they gave some control of themselves to him in their act of loving. They saw their superiors not so much as individuals with faults and moral shortcomings, but as representatives of God's providential care. When superiors are perceived as individuals – and there is no suggestion that they should not be so perceived – it becomes apparent that they are not all loveable people. The mannerisms, the personality, the attitude, the behavior of some superiors can be offensive to some of their subjects. The Sister must then relinquish control under obedience without the aid of love's persuasion. Love is somewhat threatening because it involves loss of control; obedience without love is doubly threatening because it forces some loss of control but provides little satisfaction for that loss.

The capacity for loving may be related to hereditary factors and environmental conditioning. The manner in which a person loves and expects or accepts love in return is surely related to childhood experiences. The manner in which a child encounters love or the lack of love will influence his later reactions within a love relationship. Some adults place love in a reward or punishment frame of reference. A parent may communicate to the child that she is loved only if she behaves properly. This may begin early in life. "If you keep clean you are a good little girl and Mommy will love you." "If you are well-behaved in public, we will love you and others will, too." "If you bring home a good report card . . . . If you never drink alcohol . . . . If you do this or that, we will love you." Love becomes something purchased through good behavior. A person so trained learns the bargains that can be extracted in the name of love. "If you love me, you will not question my authority, but do what I request of you." "If you love me you will be a good religious, because then I will be pleased and love you in return."

Sometimes love becomes a reward for bad behavior. The young child whose parents are too busy to give her any attention may discover that she gets a great deal of attention when she does something naughty. Attention is a poor substitute for affection, but the two can be easily confused in the mind of a child. Consider how so many unloved persons strive so hard to force the attention of others in an attempt to find their affection. The pattern of parental concern which follows problem behavior reenforces the child's attitude that this is the only method of obtaining parental involvement in her life. When the child becomes an adult, it is difficult to break the pattern. She becomes the religious who does not seem satisfied unless the superior is angry at her. She may go to great lengths to achieve this goal which is so unsatisfying. She truly tempts her superior to wrath and when she is assured of love by the superior's anger, she directs her need for love to higher authorities. The end result is a series of frustrated superiors who seem unable to provide Sister with a situation in which she can be happy, and a frustrated Sister who never finds happiness because she cannot prepare for love but can only provoke to anger.

Love which demands a kind of behavioral response on the part of the loved one is more a grasping of another than a giving of self. It is tyranny. It is control. This kind of love, if one continues to call such a relationship by that name, is not unknown in religious communities. The bartering may take new forms at present, but the bargain remains the same. "If you love me join my cause, adopt these new ideas, follow this lead which I pass on so willingly to you. Sing my songs, repeat my slogans, attend to all that my favorite authors would say to you. If you love me, if you want me to love you, discard the shackles of the past, think with me, plan with me, do as I do." This manner of loving creates a kind of medium of exchange. It is not love itself that is exchanged, but only the agreements that are transacted under the pretext of love. The relationship might be described as a mutually wary involvement between two people. It could more appropriately be called an adult business relationship, for it contains the getting and giving of words, of signs, of material things. It contains little giving of self.

Unfortunately, the level of love may not be the same for two people who are involved in the words of love. One may be responding at bargain level, but the other may be responding at gift level. The religious is accomplished in loving at gift level; otherwise she would not have become a religious. She needs to be suspicious of the bargain level of love when her own affection is being priced.

If the attitudes of love are fashioned in early years, one might ask how proper attitudes are formed. Parents who love their child *because* he is and not *for what* he is teach him the lesson of true love. Parents who love their child because he lives and not because he lives for them give him something with which to meet life. If they respond to him because he has needs to be fulfilled and not because he fulfills their needs, they will find their own need to be loved fulfilled by him. Parents who love their child enough to allow him to say, "No," to let him think for himself and make his own mistakes, will provide him with a personality capable of loving. If parents help their child develop into a mature adult capable of loving, they run the risk of his not loving them; for if he is free to love maturely then he is free not to love them. If, on the other hand, they disallow his development to the stature of mature lover, they *necessarily* incur the misfortune of his not loving them. If he is not free to love maturely, he cannot love them maturely.

There is a suitable analogy in the Sister who feels so constrained to love God. It is so necessary for her to do so. It takes so much of her effort and requires so much of her attention. She struggles constantly with the motions of love, because she approaches immaturely the notion of love. Watching her approach to love of God, one can surmise a great deal about the attitudes of love which her parents must have imparted to her.

The healthy parental attitude which has been described creates in the developing child a recognition of his own worth as a human being. He establishes an opinion of respect for himself. He can then respect others. He learns a healthy love of self and on this basis he can love others in a mature manner.

There are many forms of love as well as many disguises. There are certain characteristics of a love that is mature and healthy. First of all, it is based on respect. It is so incongruous to observe two people who profess their love for each other treat one another without respect. The person who insists on respect from others rarely is caught in a degrading relationship disguised as love. The religious who discovers love but finds lack of respect for herself as a religious may later find lack of regard for herself as a woman. Love may survive the former, but not the latter.

Mature love must not be impulsive; there must be that balance between reason and love which prevents loss of self-control. The teenage girl, in her impulsivity, states that she will die for love. And she does – by the hundreds every year. Adolescent boys also commit suicide for love. Though their love might be called infatuation, when it is coupled with their impulsivity it is potentially dangerous. An ancient proverb states, "They love too much who die for love." Love must be contained, must have its limit. That boundary is the edge of reason.

Mature love must preserve the integrity of the one who is loved. There must be a basic respect for the person and the personality; his worth as an individual, his inner freedoms should not be violated. In addition to this, his singular traits, personal attitudes, and particular needs are to be respected. Especially important is a reverential awareness of his weaknesses. Persons who love one another deeply are touched by a channel of interaction which brings each to increasing awareness of the intricacies and delicacies of the other's personality. Such awareness, which is often "unaware" awareness, permits the possibility of unkind intrusion into the recesses of another's feelings. One who loves has the possibility of inflicting pain, for love knows the frailty as well as the strength of the beloved, even though the intellect may deny that imperfections exist. One who loves must be careful not to take advantage of the other's weakness but must complement with stability and understanding this beloved counterpart of one's own imperfection.

Fully developed love not only preserves the integrity of the one who is loved but also demands the preservation of one's own integrity. The person whose love takes him beyond the exercise of reason loves hollowly because he loves less humanly. If one loses one's self-respect in loving, one loses the power of loving so much. The one who loves but sacrifices some of his integrity in the relationship may give of himself to the one he loves, but at the same time he loses part of himself. That part is lost to both the lover and the beloved. As a result, the lover has less of himself to give.

Love that is mature acts as a kind of centrifugal force within the individual. It is expansive and brings one to others. The highest ideal of love is to see oneself as a channel of divine love, the source and the goal of all love. We become, then, the mediators of love in our caring for others, not in the abstract coldness of intellectual perception, but in the warmth of emotional affinity. God's love flows through us to others. We give, then, not of ourselves in loving, but open those paths of love within us and lose nothing of ourselves in that passing.

Love is not truly quantifiable and consequently cannot be measured. It is so wrong to weigh love with words as doubting lovers do. Insistence upon statements of love can be based on mistrust of others or of oneself. The insecure need reassurance that they are loved, because they doubt their loveableness. Religious, as well as others, who doubt their attractiveness as persons may seek proof of their interpersonal merit by provoking some affectionate but imprudent attachment.

Love cannot be measured in minutes or hours even though lovers may carefully count the moments they are apart. Love is not part of time but seeks the promise of eternal commitment. The religious woman finds such a pledge in her fidelity to her own vows. She holds this eternal commitment in the power of her love as no other woman has the force to do, no matter how strong her love may be. With this eternal pledge as background, Sister still needs to complete the picture with an enduring love of religious life. This may be difficult to achieve.

Today's Sister is pushed into the center of life's stage and there, for herself and all the world to hear, must answer the question, "Whom do you love?" She cannot be content to love quietly and simply, the way she had for centuries. She cannot avoid a topic which those outside as well as inside the religious life force upon her. Now she is expected to love as if she somehow had been emotionally impotent for years. She must state her position. She must defend it. The implication is obvious that her feminine qualifications include loving. In this focus of attention it is easy to become confused. Sisters might do well to examine some of their relationships to determine whether or not they are mature love. It sometimes happens that parents push their children into imprudent love affairs and unwise marriages because they are concerned about having an unwed son or daughter in the family. Their daughter may get married to prove to them that she is not an "old maid." It is possible also for religious women to rush into some hastily contrived "love affair" for the purpose of proving they are truly women. These so-called romances may be morally innocent but emotionally damaging. They have the impulsivity and lack of depth of adolescent infatuation. The summer school romance is rarely a lasting relationship, but its disturbing influence may last considerably longer than the summer.

Many argue that unless Sister knows something about real love she cannot be genuine in her relationships with others. The Sister who is out of touch with the meaning of love is out of touch with the meaning of God, of religion, and of the religious life. It is hardly appropriate for her to serve her apprenticeship of love in some lately-contrived arrangement if she already works with the Master of Love.

Religious sometimes take a naive view of the physical side of existence. Their naiveté is indicated in their unrealistic attitude toward physical love or sexuality. Perhaps because of their training they have formed an attitude that reason must always dominate the other faculties and when it does not there is a disorder present. It is a short step from this disquieting reflection to the comfortable position of denying many of their sensory impulses. The result of such denial leaves them limited in their ability to cope with the effects of their sensory reactions. Their state of unawareness makes them vulnerable to the results of strong sensory impulses which may reach an end point before they recognize that something has definitely begun. If Sister cannot quite deny these impulses, she may attempt to disguise them in some manner. The deception has its own probability of disaster. Intense sexual interest is disguised as "natural curiosity." Sexually stimulating conversations are camouflaged as "discussions about sex." Physical contact that is erotic in purpose and result is misrepresented as "a form of communication." Indeed it is a communication. In this regard it is wise to be aware of and honest about what one is communicating.

The premise on which Sister founds her conclusions about sexuality is not quite as clear-cut in reality as it might have been in her training. Sexual feelings may occur in a manner that initially defies rational control. Other sensory reactions occur quite independently of reason and in response to various internal or external stimuli. The feelings of hunger, of anger, of nausea may all be cited as examples. The more one becomes anxious about experiencing these sensory reactions, the more likely one is to aggravate the feelings. If a Sister becomes intensely anxious the moment she experiences some erotic sensation, she is likely to increase the eroticism and decrease the possibility of moving naturally to new reactions. She focuses her attention on the sexual response, and quickly transforms it from a purely physical response to a level of intellectual interest, emotional involvement, and moral conflict.

There is an inconsistency in the behavior of the religious who sees damnation in the flame of initial sexual reaction, but who defines a highly erotic relationship as a mode of innocent communication. Either of these reactions may occur within the same Sister. They may be reactions to a person of either sex. Neurotic conflict is almost certain to occur in the religious who denies any sexual feelings because they are sordid and sinful and who, at the same time, engages in behavior which is sure to incite erotic desires.

Homosexual attraction and homosexual activity have existed, do exist and will continue to exist within religious communities. There is no evidence that religious life produces persons with homosexual tendencies. Individuals with these propensities may seek admission to the religious life, which very realistically offers them immunity from married life and, in addition, provides them with a "homosexual society" in which to live. This does not suggest by any means that religious communities are societies of homosexuals, but rather that they do represent a group of persons living together, and all of the same sex. In such a situation it is not surprising that when a Sister has a sexual feeling she may, as she focuses concern on it, believe that the object of that feeling is another Sister. In fact, it may be. This does not make Sister a homosexual. If she worries about it long enough she may find herself having similar reactions, more because she is worried about having them than because they are stimulated by external events. In any case, she will do well not to attend too carefully to these reactions lest they be magnified by her concerns. She must develop that balanced response in which she is sufficiently aware of their existence to cope with them but not so confounded by their existence to enlarge upon them.

Sisters should accept the reality that emotional impressions register in consciousness and must be dealt with as factors influencing one's ability to reason and one's opportunity to will. If a person, under extreme sensory stimulation or severe emotional response, reasons poorly and chooses imprudently, he may still be behaving perfectly. This is not perfect human behavior in an abstract sense, but perfect behavior in the real sense of being human. This does not exempt the religious from responsibility for her behavior; rather it establishes the requirement that she be alert to the reality of her own behavior and honest in her obligation to behave with propriety.

Sisters now ask questions they never dared ask before. They also ask questions which never occured before because the problem did not exist, or, if it did, they needed no query to know the answer. Some of the questions presently asked have to do with their relationships with men. Can a Sister have a romantic relationship with a priest, for example? How does she know if she is "in love?" Can she have certain physical contacts with a male friend? How far can these go? "Being in love" and "loving someone" have different connotations. The first suggests an emotional involvement with a diminution of rational control and a tendency to progress to physical exchanges. The second suggests greater rational control, an emotional involvement of a limited degree, as well as a level of relationship capable of existing independently of a physical basis. According to these definitions, Sister has every right to "love someone" but no right to "be in love" with someone. This is analogous to the married woman who may love other men than her husband but who has no right to be in love with any one of them. The statement that a Sister should fall in love at some time so that she can love others is ridiculous. One need not fall out of an airplane to appreciate the pleasure of flying.

God is love. The religious approaches God in a way others do not. Although perhaps only culturally determined, men are considered to be governed more by reason, women by emotion. Religious women know God and know love; they cannot love perfectly, but they can love in a way others cannot. They should not strive to love as others do, but strive to teach others to love as women of religion are capable of doing. They should be what they are – women of God, women of love; not too far removed from others so that when they hurt, the Sister will suffer with them and soothe them, so that when others are lonely, the Sister will not isolate them but through her presence lead them to God, so that when others are afraid the Sister will illumine them with her vision and reassure them with the truth of her life.

CHAPTER X

FULFILLMENT OF THE FEMININE PERSONALITY IN THE RELIGIOUS LIFE

In the unknown course of life, it is natural to look for a charted path, a "known" way. The parental task includes a great deal of guidance for the young. The Church gives us wise counsel in matters spiritual. The state has many directives which regulate our temporal lives. Society has unwritten laws of propriety to which we all conform. In all these areas there are regulations which act as guidelines, ideals which serve as models. It is not too difficult to draw a mental picture of a good citizen, a good Catholic, a good neighbor, a good person.

The situation is far different when we attempt to describe a good personality or a healthy manner of adjustment. In religious matters, in civil affairs, the rules take precedence and the individual must be trimmed to fit the garment. In psychological processes, the lines are not so sharply drawn, the rules are not so clearly stated. Here the individual is supreme; he is the author of his own autonomy, the designer of his own adjustment. Personality development is uniquely differentiated. Personality adaptation is highly individualized. Personality fulfillment is accomplished solitarily.

One sees immediately an apparent incompatability in the two concepts of this chapter title. Personality fulfillment implies a freedom of activity, a latitude of development, a wide range of choice. It also suggests a highly individualized adjustment to the complexities of one's environment. The religious life, on the other hand, stresses conformity to rule, submission of self, suppression of individuality. Thus, one sees that this life of the religious presents a new duality that is a struggle between individuality and conformity, a conflict between expression and submission.

The young woman who enters religion brings much with her. She leaves her worldly possessions behind, but she cannot leave behind those experiences which she stores within her heart. In her investiture ceremony she can discard her worldly clothing and receive the special garments of her chosen state. But she cannot be stripped of her psychological coverings. She cannot leave outside the threshold of the community the fabric of her past from which her personality has been fashioned. She can separate herself from the physical presence of her family and friends, but she cannot separate herself psychologically from their past influence.

So, truly, the young novice brings much with her when she enters religion. She brings her own humanity and all the needs her human nature has in common with others. In addition, she brings her own treasured memories, her own guarded secrets, her own special experiences, her own private ambitions and dreams, her own various loves. All of this is the legacy of life which the young religious aspirant must guard with courage lest it be lost to her. She must develop it with wisdom that it may bring dividends of satisfaction, of grace, and of eternity.

To fulfill her personality in religion cannot mean, therefore, to forget the past, because the past is a constant part of her. To fulfill her personality in religion cannot mean to ignore the present, because through the present she must find satisfactions for her needs. From the past come two kinds of needs; those common to all, and those special needs arising from the particular temperament and special experiences of the individual. This final chapter will be concerned only with common needs.

The person entering religion gives herself to God, but the needs which she brings with her are a sort of divine dowry which God gives the community. This uncut and unpolished stone may have many flaws, or it may be a jewel of great excellence. It comes from God; it is the product of his hand. But the process of cutting and polishing it remains the work of the individual and the community. Only God knows the potential for perfection of each stone. The individual religious can only strive to perfect the diamond of self by satisfying or sublimating the many facets that are represented by her multiple needs. A religious dedication, an emptying of self, a spirit of detachment cannot leave this entourage of needs behind, for they are part of self. Leave them behind and one is destined to remain incomplete. Attempt to destroy them and one may suddenly find them operating independently and dangerously, that is, outside of conscious control.

The fulfillment of personality and the life of a religious are not incompatible. They are, in fact, in deepest harmony for the religious life must be lived in an individual way if it is to be more than the hollow echo of the foundress' voice sounding down through the centuries. The spiritual life is not the termination, but the culmination of individual personality fulfillment. Self cannot be obliterated. Consider the personality of the different saints. Each of them loved God as everyone should love him. But didn't they do it in some of the strangest, most individual ways imaginable?

There are communities in which personality fulfillment is very difficult because individuality is sharply suppressed. I think these are the exception and are becoming even rarer. There are communities in which Sisters seem to come off an assembly line, rather than out of a novitiate. They act alike, talk alike, laugh alike, (or more probably refrain from laughter in the same manner). Sometimes they even look alike.

Some of this assembly line atmosphere seeps into many communities. The rule becomes overemphasized. It is called the holy rule and then becomes almost a part of dogma. The individual begins to exist solely for the community. One wonders if that's the way it should be. There is such a thing as the common good, but this concept must be weighed carefully in its application. Think of what Hitler did to the Jews for the "common good." Think of what some people in the South have done to the Negroes for the "common good." When a Sister begins to exist solely for the community she is consumed by the rigidity of the rule rather than by her own spontaneous love of God. The Sister who is poured into a mold becomes rigid within herself, inflexible with others.

It is certainly true that the religious woman who fulfills her own psychological needs broadens her personality and her charity, enriches herself and her faith. She is a better religious because she is a healthier person. She fills more of her spiritual potential because she is fulfilled.

What are some of the common needs which a woman has and how can these be realized within the framework of religious vows? These needs have been variously classified and there are long lists available. It should be sufficient to discuss the following ones briefly: the need to be oneself, the need to be worthwhile, the need to accomplish, the need to serve and to surrender, the need to grow, the need to relax and recreate, the need to love and to be loved, the need for privacy.

It may seem self-evident to say that one needs to be oneself. It is not always so self-evident, nor is it always possible to be oneself easily. One of the goals of psychotherapy is helping people to be themselves, to realize what they are really like; it is only after this goal is reached that one can talk meaningfully of change. The question might be asked, "How could I be other than what I am?" And the answer is that the world is full of simulation, and the religious, too, must hide behind many different masks at times. What about the religious who must pretend she is perfect, either to herself or to others, or both? What about the Sister who, for the sake of the community, must pretend that she is happy and content when, indeed, she is most troubled? What about the Sister who is constantly putting on an act as she goes through the motions of being a Sister, when deep inside she doubts that she ever should have become a Sister? What about the Sister who is frightened of suffering, of ill health, of possible war, of family disaster? She is really frightened but cannot tell anyone how she, who must put her supernatural trust in God, can be so naturally terrified.

This strain to be other than what they are becomes insupportable for some. How else can we explain it when some religious who was a model to everyone, an exemplary religious, suddenly breaks with reality and is whisked away to a mental hospital, or as suddenly breaks with her vows and disappears, leaving behind the aftermath of shocked whispers. It seems to happen suddenly, without warning. The person seems to change completely, abruptly. The fact is she was not being herself, and appeared to have no problems when she had some grievous ones indeed.

Most people accept the fact that individuals must maintain an exterior pose which they present to the world. It would not be fitting for a religious to speak of her imperfections openly, to broadcast her unhappiness or discontent publicly. The point is that she should be allowed to have these deficiencies, to experience these feelings, and to acknowledge to herself that she has them. Perhaps, at times, it may be necessary to speak of them quietly to another, be it a spiritual director, a superior, a friend, relative, or a doctor; as long as it is someone with a gentle ear.

That is what is meant by the need to be oneself. It is to be weak when inner strength is gone, to be afraid when the darkness of the unknown clutches at the heart, to be sad when the beauty of life is closeted behind a narrow view. It is also to be generous, to be kind. But these will come when one can be oneself in baser ways.

After the need to be oneself comes the need to be worthwhile. This is the priceless heritage that parents should pass on to their children. It cannot depend on what one accomplishes, for the rich and the poor, the wise and the stupid, the saint and the sinner is each one worthwhile. It is based on the intrinsic worth of a human being, whether that human being is a fetus in its mother's womb, a crippled child who will never walk or talk, a genius of the intellectual world, or a giant of the spiritual world. Some who are not convinced of their own personal worth enter religion in order to become worthwhile, in the hope that the contagion of sanctity will save them from their own unworthiness. However, a feeling of personal worth is a prerequisite of adult psychology. No degree of industry, no measure of accomplishment is adequate to prove the intrinsic value of an individual. Each community has one or more of those religious who can never do enough, who are never satisfied with what they do or with themselves. They can never relax; they need to be busy. There is a ceaselessness in their work that makes others uneasy; there is a restless passion in it that makes others uncomfortable. They are almost self-destructive in their frenzy to accomplish the impossible, i.e., to establish their own personal worth. Indeed, their plight reminds us of the moth and the candle.

This personality need to be worthwhile cannot, therefore, be fulfilled by the religious life alone. It can be fulfilled in the religious life, but it must be consummated within the little workshop of one's mind, not within the framework of community living.

Another common need is the need to be useful to others, the need to contribute of oneself. This is, at least externally, fulfilled in the religious life, for the Sister's life usually involves a dedication of self to the service of others, either in teaching or in the care of the sick, the orphaned, the aged, the derelict. However, this need to be useful must not only *be* fulfilled, but the religious must *realize* that it is fulfilled. The Sister who has lost the vision of her sacred vows, the perspective of her noble purpose, sees only the sacrifice she makes daily in her classroom and not the reward of the future when the seeds of faith and love she sows in children's hearts will blossom with the glory of the Resurrection. As Sister makes her weary rounds in the hospital or orphanage, or spends long, lonely hours in the thankless toil of administration, she sees only the work which increases faster than it is accomplished. To see beyond the disease and dirt which are the object of her daily chores, to see beyond the desk which seems to imprison her, Sister must meditate. Whether it be on her knees at 5 A.M., or as she walks the path of duty through the day, she must reflect on the unseen goodness of what she does.

There is little immediate gratification in washing the dirty hands of orphans, caring for the diseased bodies of the sick and the aged, instructing students in arithmetic, or even religion. The same is true for the married woman who cannot see a soul behind her child's dirty face or hear the whisper of her own heart within the noisy backwash of her offspring. Only meditation of some sort brings the mother and the nun to a realization of the hidden grandeur of their womanhood.

A woman's need to accomplish takes a special form which is characteristic of her sex; she has the need to be of service to others and the need to surrender. The married woman obviously reaches fulfillment in this by her role of service in the family, by her surrender of self. It is the woman who feels enslaved in the home, trapped within the confines of her marriage, who comes to resent her lot. Similarly, the religious who feels she is *a servant in* the community rather than *of service to* the community, who considers herself trapped by the obligations of her vows, rather than challenged by the privilege of her commitment – it is this religious who comes to resent her fate.

Surrender brings a woman to the peak of fulfillment. It is often unwillingness to surrender that makes a married woman physically frigid, psychologically frustrated in her role of wife and mother. The religious who finds the courage to surrender her own desires to the demands of the life she has freely chosen finds herself gloriously fulfilled. The thread of sacrifice runs through the cloth of everyone's life. If the stitching is guided by thoughtful meditation the thread can become a golden pattern which makes the garment of life beautiful. If it is left to the random influence of external events, it scars and mars the integrity of life's design.

The religious has a need to grow, to progress, to move ahead psychologically. Humans seek happiness; by nature they must do so. Since they do not have complete happiness at any one moment, of necessity they must continue to search for it, to look for something better. It is not right to be too content; that is the reason psychiatrists say that some anxiety is necessary. Without it a person would cease to grow. This is not an attempt to extol the discontent or to condone the malcontent. But a certain restlessness gives inner growth.

Lay women are encouraged to improve themselves in different areas. They are encouraged to read widely. They are encouraged to become interested in politics, in international affairs, in the theater, in community problems. They are advised to develop hobbies, to paint, to knit, to sew, to collect coins, to weave baskets. These things are not suggested simply so they can fill their idle hours. They are suggested so they can fulfill themselves by developing their minds, increasing their skills, enlarging their interests in life. It is no longer bold to suggest that religious have hobbies, that they be encouraged to read widely, watch a little more TV at times, learn about and argue politics, become familiar with the theater, the arts, to get interested in various community affairs. Why shouldn't Sister march in civil rights demonstrations? Unless she lives in a contemplative order, the time has passed when Sister can be sheltered from the world. The world needs to feel her compassion, and she needs to be touched by the pain that is in the world.

This brings us to another need which must be fulfilled if personality is to be complete. The religious, like everyone else, has the need to relax, to recreate. There are many psychological limitations in religious life. Recreation is probably the most limited. It is true that community life can deprive an individual of any real recreation, for recreation is largely a personal matter. What relaxes one makes another tense. What recreates one, bores another. One cannot legislate leisure or regulate relaxation.

There are various possibilities to enlarge the range of recreational opportunities. A free range of conversation at meal time, at least, may do much to improve community disposition, as well as individual digestion. Eating together is fundamentally a social act. But the social aspect is completely dampened when people stare blankly at one another, or even worse, contain their eyes within the limits of their plate as a voice drones on through the drudgery of spiritual reading. A little laughter seasons food well. A little conversation cheers the heart and warms the stomach. It is second best to a glass of wine with meals. To have both conversation and wine would be even better!

Even in this time of change, recreation in some convents means sitting around in a circle, waiting for the superior to speak so that one can reply "Yes, Mother," or "No, Mother." This can hardly be relaxing. The more spontaneous and varied recreation is, the more it will answer the individual's need to relax. Recreation is aimed at relaxing the whole person, the psychosomatic unit. It should relax the mind by providing a change of pace, a variation of interest, a new focus. In addition, it should relax the body by providing an opportunity for physical activity, an outlet for physical energy. It would be excellent if every convent could be equipped with a full gymnasium, including a punching bag, and a swimming pool. These are a bit expensive. In the meantime, roller skating or square dancing in the basement allows for change from mental strain and physical inactivity. Many religious have more physical activity than they need. Is there any reason why these can't just lounge and chat with someone during recreation, or play a game of bridge or even poker, or read a good book? How many religious have cards at the local public library and use them regularly? Or the physically tired religious might like to go to her room and take a nap. Or she might like to watch something on television besides the news. There are days when the news is not very relaxing.

Others can escape the pressures of their life in many healthy ways. Clergy go out for a drive, go to a movie, go visit a friend. Husbands and wives go out for the evening because they get tired of the confinement in the narrow cloister of their home. How about some ecumenical spirit in the religious life? Why couldn't communities invite one another for an evening get-together, maybe a bingo game, or how about a hootenanny?

The proper use of leisure time is important in life adjustment and is the hallmark of a stable, mature person.

Sister has a need to love and to be loved. She has these needs in the natural as well as the supernatural order. They are not satisfied by the intellectual virtue of charity; these are the emotional needs to give and to receive affection. St. Thomas said that man is a social animal. Loneliness is truly a cross that each person must bear in his own manner, but friendship and love make the burden lighter.

The closest bonds in life are those of blood, and good relatives help protect us from the weaknesses and wickedness within ourselves. Although the religious must leave her family to become a Sister, she should not leave them out of her life. It is not an unusual reaction for modern parents to resent a daughter's decision to enter the convent. They sometimes say, "It will be as if she is dead." Why do they react this way? Are they afraid that their daughter will become emotionally dead, that she will not love them any more? It seems to work that way sometimes. Their vibrant young daughter, full of life and fun and enthusiasm, goes off to the convent. Each time they visit her, they see her sparkle dimming into a pious pose, her laughter changing into a saintly smile. The enthusiastic kiss she used to give them is now a careful handshake without too much pressure, of course. Sister is becoming holy in novitiate, and a holy person must guard against sensory or worldly pleasure because therein lies temptation. The words "sensual" and "sensuous" ought to take their rightful place as dignified descriptive adjectives of a very proper part of our nature, just as things intellectual or spiritual are. Religious training should give some consideration to the healthy development and gratification of the sensual side of the person. Psychiatry is not opposed to self-denial or to sacrifice. In fact, it is known to be a law of life. But it cannot be denied that one has a body with various sense organs and God has provided many legitimate ways of fulfilling them.

A religious needs the continuing affection of her family and of her friends outside the community. She should maintain it by visiting them and having them visit her. She should maintain it by letters and phone calls. Within the community she needs the affection of new friends, and a basic fact of life ought to be recognized – that in any group of people, the individual will find some she likes better than others, and she will want to form close ties with a few. It is time to be honest. Everyone has special friends. The relationship should not be maligned by suggesting that there is something sordid in liking one person more than others. However, fraternal charity and the concerns of community life necessitate an association with all, so special friendships must not become exclusive.

In addition to these relationships, a Sister will frequently establish some association with lay people, perhaps parents or her students or patients from her hospital. Such relationships ought not be scrutinized too closely. Why should there be the constant fear that sister might run off with someone? She has dedicated her life to God; she can certainly be trusted to talk to a layman.

Finally, Sister, like all other mortals, has a need for privacy. She needs the privacy of her own mind, and surely she cannot have it if she constantly feels harassed by the perpetual presence of other community members. She needs the privacy of her own person, and surely she cannot have it if she has no decent separate room to which she can retire. She needs the privacy of communication with her superior, with her confessor, with her friends and family. Mail need not be censored. If she is planning an elopment she will likely never discuss it in her letters. She needs the privacy of communication with her physician even though he may be physician to her superior and to the rest of the community. So often a Sister goes to a doctor and is not allowed to be alone with him, even for his history taking. When he has finished his examination, he sometimes hands the prescription to the superior and says, "Have Sister take one of these after every meal." And Sister, who is being treated like a five year old, is sitting there before him. He really ought to give her a lollipop.

The terrors of solitary confinement have long been understood by humans. Men have learned a new technique of torture: to have someone watching you twenty-four hours a day. Reflect on it a moment. This must be maddening. The human need for privacy is just as strong and just as important as is the human need for companionship.

Although the following part of a poem does not, in any way, encompass the wealth of dedication of the religious life, it suggests an interesting background of natural fulfillment on which one might consider building a spiritual superstructure.

> "He who has gained the respect of intelligent men and the
> love of little children,
> Who has left the world better than he found it,
> Whether by an improved poppy, a perfect poem, or a rescued soul,
> He who has lived well, laughed often, and loved much,
> He has achieved success."